ALL SHALL BE WELL

*A bereavement anthology
and companion*

JOAN WILSON

with

ALF McCREARY

CANTERBURY
PRESS
Norwich

© Joan Wilson and Alf McCreary 2001

Bible quotations are taken from the New International Version,
published in Great Britain by Hodder and Stoughton, 1982

First published in 2001 by The Canterbury Press Norwich
(a publishing imprint of Hymns Ancient & Modern Limited
a registered charity)
St Mary's Works, St Mary's Plain
Norwich, Norfolk, NR3 3BH
Paperback edition 2008

British Library Cataloguing in Publication data

A catalogue record of this book is available from the British Library

ISBN 978-1-85311-932-3

Typeset by Rowland Phototypesetting Ltd,
Bury St Edmunds, Suffolk
and printed in Great Britain by
MPG Books Ltd,
Bodmin, Cornwall

Contents

Foreword

On 8 November 1987, the townspeople of Enniskillen in County Fermanagh gathered at the local Cenotaph for the Remembrance Day service. It never took place. Shortly before 11am, an IRA bomb ripped apart a disused school. The intended target had been the security forces, but instead the bomb killed eleven civilian people, and many others were injured – some of them terribly so.

Gordon Wilson and his daughter Marie, a twenty-year-old student nurse, were buried in a heap of rubble. They held hands and comforted each other until Marie lost consciousness. Before she did so, Marie squeezed Gordon's hand and said, 'Daddy, I love you very much.' Those were the last words she spoke. She died several hours later in the local Erne Hospital. Gordon was rescued and treated for a dislocated shoulder, and cuts and bruising.

That evening, still dazed and in pain, he spoke to a BBC reporter who asked him for a brief comment, following such an immense tragedy. Gordon's words became part of the history of the best and the worst of Northern Ireland. He said: 'I bear no ill-will, I bear no grudge. Dirty sort of talk is not going to bring her back to life. Don't ask me, please, for a purpose. I don't have a purpose. I don't have an answer. But I know there has to be a plan . . . It's part of a greater plan, and God is good. And we shall meet again.'

His words went around the world and touched a universal human chord. He was to become a local and national celebrity, something which worried him deeply. A natural in front of a microphone, he was sought out by a media hungry for sound-bites.

In a very short time he became a household name. He was commended by the Queen in her Christmas Day broadcast that year, he was acknowledged as one of the most courageous voices to bring hope and forgiveness out of the depths of despair, and following an offer from the Irish Prime Minister Albert Reynolds, he became an independent Senator in the Parliament in Dublin – a position he used to good effect to speak out against violence. Tragically, he died from a heart attack on 27 June 1995, when he still had so much to do and to say.

The Enniskillen bombing did more than rip apart a disused building. It also destroyed the lives of eleven innocent people in and around Enniskillen, in the same way that the violence of Northern Ireland has killed, maimed and tortured countless people over the past thirty years and more.

This is the story of the Wilson family, and particularly the story of Joan Wilson in her own words, which she hopes and prays will be of help to others suffering bereavement. It is a book to be read at your own pace, in your particular times of need. You may find a word, a sentence or a passage which may bring comfort, and which may enable you to move through the worst of the darkness to a time and a place where you may again be able to catch a glimpse of the light. That is why Joan herself chose the title of this book, 'All Shall Be Well'.

During my research for my book on Marie and a subsequent book on Gordon himself, I came to know the Wilson family extremely well. I admired the strength and courage of each one of them, and none more than that of Joan herself. She was a rock for Gordon and her entire family, and that rock was founded and grounded on a deep Christian faith which brought her through the depths of loss and despair. The words of Joan in this book are the authentic voice of the bereaved, moving through the valley of death and, most important, to something that lies beyond it. There are few people of such depth and experience to guide you on this journey. I commend this book to all who are searching for words of comfort and of hope in their time of need.

Alf McCreary
May 2001

MARIE

The Loss of Innocence

On the evening of 25 September 1987 we had gathered together in the family home in Cooper Crescent, Enniskillen, to celebrate Gordon's sixtieth birthday. Our eldest child and only son, Peter, then in the family business with his father, was present with his wife Ingrid and their two daughters Eloise (4) and Judith (2). Our elder daughter Julie-Anne, who was a primary school teacher, and our younger daughter Marie, who was completing her second year in nursing training in the Royal Victoria Hospital, Belfast, had arranged the party. It was an evening of fun, happiness and gentle teasing. We all joked 'Father is now sixty – he's over the hill!' Gordon was a keen golfer, though hardly of Ryder Cup standard, but he loved being out on the course. So we gave him an electric golf trolley to make his round of golf easier!

I felt very relaxed and happy on that evening. I was thankful to have my loved ones around me, thankful to have them settled in their chosen careers and delighted with the little grandchildren. Little did I realize it was to be our last happy family gathering before a fiery trial.

At this period I was very happy in my own job teaching violin in various schools around the area. I loved teaching and making music with children and I was delighted in having two granddaughters who also shared my love for music. A few weeks before this party I had read and reflected on a lovely piece in Peter Scott's book, *Eye on the Wind*.

I am without question the luckiest and I believe the happiest man I know. I think I am lucky because I am loved by the woman to whom this book is dedicated, because I can spend my time and earn my living doing the things I most enjoy, because I was born with a happy disposition.

Not that I have not known misery or despair. I am given to moods, but they do not last long because life is *too* short to let them spoil my enjoyment. I think enjoyment is a glorious bonus not as something I am entitled to as right. My enjoyment is positive – a delight in being alive and sharing my enthusiasms with others and particular delight in the natural world around me.[1]

Many of us can identify with these beautiful words. Contentment is one of life's greatest blessings, but the harsh reality is that none of us can experience unbroken happiness throughout our lives. The deep happiness I felt in those early weeks in the autumn of 1987 was to be cruelly shattered not once, but again and again through the loss of my younger daughter, my only son and my beloved husband, and all within a short space of time. Looking back it seems like a loss of innocence from those earlier days of bliss.

This small book is a record of my intimate thoughts and feelings during those dreadful, turbulent days of irreplaceable loss, and my slow, painful journey in learning to cope with bereavement and to move from the darkness towards a glimpse of the light. It is my hope and prayer that these words will help you as you make that journey also.

The Calm Before the Storm

There was, I recall, another lovely experience which I shared with Marie and which I will never forget. It was a few weeks after Gordon's birthday party and Marie was home from Belfast for a short break. It was the autumn half term and Marie and I decided to go to Donegal. On a crisp, dry, sunny autumn day we drove to the Fanad Peninsula. The scenery was magical, and I was so happy in my daughter's company. She loved Donegal, the deserted beaches, the sheep wandering on the roadside, and the wide, expansive sky. One of the loveliest aspects of Donegal is the feeling of freedom amid such beauty. We were totally relaxed, and felt at one with God's beautiful creation. I spoke aloud these beautiful words from one of my favourite hymns by Isaac Watts, 'I sing the almighty power of God'.

> I sing the goodness of the Lord
> That filled the earth with food:
> He formed the creatures with His word
> And then pronounced them good.
>
> Lord, how thy wonders are displayed
> Where'er I turn my eye,
> If I survey the ground I tread
> Or gaze upon the sky.

This was an unforgettable treasure of a day, with this beauty and perfection all around us. Yet amid this serenity and happiness, almost like a shadow over the sun, I felt a sudden sense of foreboding that such happiness could not last. It was something which made me draw my breath sharply, but I did not mention it to Marie. In retrospect, it was perhaps a premonition, and I was to discover only too soon that it was our last outing together. A week later Marie was killed by an IRA bomb.

I often think about that almost perfect day in Donegal. Was it a gift from God that gave us those final beautiful, intimate moments together as a mother and daughter? Was it something to hold on to, to give me not only happy memories, but also the strength to face the terrible days ahead, which, thankfully, I was not to know about at the time?

I treasure the memory of that day; it makes me thankful for all the happy times I shared with Marie, and that moment of foreboding was in its way a strange mercy, preparing me for the devastation of losing her.

Maybe you have had a similar experience. Perhaps it is guidance from God to live every moment, to drink in the fullness of the Divine creation and His provision. Christ said to us, 'Take no thought for the morrow', and exhorted us to take heed of the reality that 'Sufficient to the day is the evil thereof.'

The Storm Breaks

On the morning of 8 November 1987, Gordon and Marie set off to the Remembrance Day Service at the Cenotaph in Enniskillen. I waved goodbye as they drove away from home to the Cenotaph. I thought, 'I shall see them after church.' It was a normal family day, though Remembrance Sunday was special to us. Gordon always made a point of going to the Cenotaph, partly because my father had served in the First World War and had lost a leg. Gordon often said to me that going to the Cenotaph each Remembrance Day, in person, was his way of saying 'Thanks' to his friends and others who had risked life and limb, some of whom had never come back.

It was a damp and dull day as Gordon and Marie left the house. I called out to her, 'Have you an umbrella?' She replied, 'Of course I have, don't fuss.' That was typically Marie! Little did I think that those would be the last words I would hear her say.

Once they left, I busied myself about the house getting ready to play the organ at the local Methodist Church, which I did every Sunday. I was glad on this particular day that I did not have to prepare a meal, as we were looking forward to lunch with my son Peter and daughter-in-law Ingrid in their home. It was always a joy to visit them and our little grand-daughters, Eloise and Judith. Tragically, the day turned out to be very different to what any of us had expected.

I found out later that as Gordon and Marie took their position in front of the wall of a disused building, an IRA bomb exploded inside, causing the wall to fall on the people below. Marie and Gordon were trapped in the rubble, and the bomb caused widespread death and mutilation. It was horrible, horrible, horrible. Even now I can hardly bear to think about it.

A long time afterwards, Gordon described what happened in his book *Marie*, which he wrote with Alf McCreary, and I have never heard or read a more graphic description of human beings being caught up in a bomb blast.

> Marie was on my right. I must have realised that the bomb had gone off behind me, and I remember seeing the wall cracking up. This all happened in a split second, but it seemed at the time as if everything was happening in slow motion, like a television replay.
>
> It was like being pushed down on my face in slow motion, it was extraordinary really. Certainly it was all happening, or seemed to be happening, slowly enough to give me time to think yet again 'My God, we're in a bomb blast ... but it can't be, not here, not at the Cenotaph on Remembrance Sunday!'
>
> Then, almost by magic, I found my hand being squeezed beneath that pile of rubble, and I knew it was Marie. But the noise outside, up there if you like, was increasing, and with all the screaming and the din and the noise, we had to shout louder and louder to make ourselves understood to each other.

Gordon kept shouting to Marie, and she assured him that she was all right. But she screamed several times, and that worried Gordon desperately. He could not figure why she was screaming, if she was saying that she was all right. But then, suddenly, the tone of her voice changed.

'She sounded different. She held my hand tightly, and gripped me as hard as she could. She said, "Daddy, I love you very much." Those were her exact words to me, and those were the last words I ever heard her say. Her hand slipped away, and we lost touch.'

The Lord Gives, the Lord Takes Away

I was in the kitchen at home when I heard a dull thud. Peter had just left, after drinking coffee with me, and I was washing the cups before going to church. I wondered whether the thud had been the noise of Peter banging his car loudly, or whether it had been a bomb. That's how many of the bombs had sounded in the past – not a deafening roar, but just a dull thud. Peter returned a short time later and told me that there had been an explosion at the Cenotaph.

We knew that Gordon and Marie had been attending the Remembrance Day service, and we were worried about their safety. When I reached our church, the minister, the Reverend Tom Magowan, sensed my anxiety and asked if I wanted to play the organ, or stay in the body of the church. I decided to play the organ because it would occupy my mind. But after about twenty minutes I could not continue. My anxiety was too great.

Then a member of the security forces, who was also a church member, told me that Gordon was in hospital with a broken arm. I asked him about Marie, but he had no news of her. My anxiety increased sharply. Peter returned and drove me to the Erne Hospital. He confirmed that Gordon was there with a broken arm, but there was no news about Marie. Julie-Anne had no news either. I began to fear the worst, and I started to cry.

The scene of distress and confusion at the hospital was like nothing I had experienced before, nor, I hope, I will ever experience again. The shock was far greater than I can possibly describe. Some people were very disturbed and were crying bitterly. Others were sobbing quietly into themselves. Yet others were trying to comfort people, and to bring what help they could.

We heard that Gordon was in the Casualty Department, and I was taken to see him. To my dismay, he was sitting in a wheelchair, and suffering great pain and discomfort. As he talked the best he could, I began to piece together some of the details of the horror following the explosion. I listened with a sense almost of disbelief as I was told that a number of people had been killed and that others were missing. I knew some of them, and the feeling of loss and tragedy was already unbearable.

In the midst of all this, we still could get no news about Marie. After hours of searching, which seemed like an eternity, we were told she was in theatre, and that she was very seriously ill. Terror seized me. I prayed, 'Lord, I have never been in a situation like this before. PLEASE HELP me, God be my strength and refuge.'

I had no track of time passing, but it must have been about 3.30pm when Marie was moved out of the operating theatre and into Intensive Care. We were brought to her. I remember praying as I walked along the corridor, 'Lord, please bring good out of this terrible, terrible evil.' On the way into Intensive Care I met a lady doctor who had lost her own daughter of twenty-seven, through cancer. She embraced me and said, 'Please God, you won't lose your daughter.' I thought immediately of the great sorrow she had suffered and how brave she had been. I prayed that this wouldn't be me. On the way into Intensive Care I was told by the nursing sister, 'Marie's heart is still beating, but it could stop at any minute.' Her words cut through me like a knife. I felt numb and helpless.

Peter, Julie-Anne and I were around Marie's bed and we could see that her life was ebbing away. A consultant doctor looked at us with great sadness, as he shook his head. I could not take it in that Marie was so terribly injured. We were still in a state of disbelief. Only a few hours earlier she had been a strong, healthy young woman on her way to the Cenotaph with her Dad.

But I knew tragically that my Marie was dying. I kissed her and I shall always see her eyelids flickering, to my dying day. The nursing sister at the bed whispered very gently, 'Mrs Wilson, Marie's heart has stopped beating.' Julie-Anne, so full of her own grief, took my hand gently and said, 'Mum, it is better this way.'

I felt the blood draining from me as my strength ebbed away. I knew that I had to depend totally on the Lord's strength. Somehow a verse from the Bible came into my consciousness, and I whispered quietly the words from Deuteronomy, 'The Lord gave, the Lord has taken away, Blessed be the name of the Lord.'

Marie, my daughter to whom I had brightly said 'Cheerio!' only that morning, was gone from our presence. My darling child, the sister of Peter and Julie-Anne, was dead. We were shocked, our world had been turned completely upside down. How could I tell my husband that his beloved daughter was dead?

I left the room, but I cannot remember making my way downstairs to Gordon, I was in such a state of shock. I do remember him asking me, 'How's Marie?' I put my arm round him gently and said, 'Our child is dead.' He cried out, 'Oh, my God, is Marie dead?' At that stage, further words failed me, but I noticed my poppy lying forlornly on the floor under Gordon's bed. This was a Remembrance Day which we would remember with great pain for the rest of our lives.

Eventually Gordon was allowed to go home. We pushed him in the wheelchair towards Peter's car. I was sick at heart because I could not bear to face going back to a home without Marie. When I think of it now, I still get that awful sick feeling in the pit of my stomach, but I also cling to the challenging and comforting words of the 23rd Psalm which, for me, has so much to say about life, and death and the life to come:

The Lord is my Shepherd; I shall not want.

He maketh me to lie down in green pastures:
he leadeth me beside the still waters.

He restoreth my soul: he leadeth me in the paths of righteousness for his name's sake.

Yea, though I walk through the valley of the shadow of death, I will fear no evil: for thou art with me; thy rod and thy staff they comfort me . . .

Surely goodness and mercy shall follow me all the days of my life: and I will dwell in the house of the Lord for ever.

The Longest Night

What kind of night would follow the awful happenings of the day? I can only describe it as a night of torment. Reeling from shock and disbelief one could not lie down or even think of sleep. I was unable to pray or utter a word. I felt desperate dreading the daylight and the future without this beloved child. I ached for my grieving wounded husband and son and daughter left without their sister, my little grand-daughters without a much-loved aunt of twenty. Darkness and despair enveloped me. I could not pray.

Next morning I was unable to hold anything in my hand, incapable of preparing breakfast or even eating. Good neighbours and friends rallied round and messages of sympathy began pouring in. I was even incapable of reading the messages. Then I heard Gordon's statement from the previous night on the radio, and reality began to set in. I heard his voice telling the story and quoting Marie's last words, 'Daddy, I love you very much', and he went on to say:

> The hospital was magnificent, truly impressive, and our friends have been great, but I have lost a daughter, and we shall miss her. But I bear no ill-will, I bear no grudge. Dirty sort of talk is not going to bring her back to life. She was a great wee lassie. She loved her profession. She was a pet. She's dead. She's in Heaven, and we'll meet again. Don't ask me, please, for a purpose. I don't have a purpose. I don't have an answer. But I know there has

to be a plan. If I didn't think that I would commit suicide. It's part of a greater plan, and God is good. And we shall meet again.

I stood rooted to the ground as I listened to his words. They were typical of him, I thought, and how right he was, but I felt anger towards those who had planted that bomb. That was something I would have to wrestle with in my own way.

This poem in beautiful italic writing was sent to us from Magee's tweed shop in Donegal. Marie and I had visited the shop ten days before the bomb. I felt this poem tied up with what Gordon had said. It has helped me greatly.

> My life is but a weaving
> Between the Lord and me
> I cannot choose the colours
> He worketh steadily
>
> Oft times He weaveth sorrow
> And I in my foolish pride
> Forget He sees the upper
> And I the under side
>
> Not till the loom is silent
> And the shuttles cease to fly
> Shall God unroll the canvas
> And explain the reason why
>
> The dark threads are as needful
> In the weaver's skilful hand
> As the threads of gold and silver
> In the pattern He has planned
>
> He knows, He loves, He cares
> Nothing this truth can dim

> He gives the very best to those
> Who leave the choice with Him.

Before Marie's earthly remains were removed from the Erne Hospital, her coffin was given a guard of honour by young student nurses. It showed how thoughtful they were, and I was deeply moved. Marie's remains were laid to rest overnight in our dearly loved Enniskillen Methodist Church where she had been baptized, and had attended Sunday School and Sunday worship. I sat dazed, numbed. I could not cry as I saw the coffin placed in the front of the communion rail. I gradually felt the peace of the building enveloping me. I heard the lovely words from John 14, verses 1–4.

> Do not let your hearts be troubled. Trust in God, trust also in me. In my Father's house are many rooms; if it were not so, I would have told you. I am going there to prepare a place for you. And if I go and prepare a place for you, I will come back and take you to be with me that you also may be where I am. You know the way to the place where I am going.

I began to feel God's comfort, and as we rose to leave the church the organist played that beautiful hymn by Anna Laetitia Waring (1820–1910):

> In Heavenly love abiding
> No change my heart shall fear;
> And safe is such confiding,
> For nothing changes here;
> The storm may roar without me,
> My heart may low be laid;
> But God is round about me
> And can I be dismayed?

Marie's Funeral

The night before Marie's funeral, we hardly slept at all, because we were worrying about the next day. We knew that the church would be packed and that there would be television cameras and reporters outside. Ours was a very private grief, and yet we had to share it in public with people from all walks of life who were grieving with us, in their own way. It was an ordeal, but it was comforting to know that we had such support.

The service was simple, moving and dignified. Marie's coffin was at the front, adorned with the family flowers. There was a sense of deep emotion in the church. Many of Marie's nursing friends and school chums were in the congregation. There were also quite a number of leading clergymen and public figures present, as well as doctors and nurses from the hospital who had fought so heroically to save lives, to bind up the wounds of the injured, and to try to bring comfort and hope to relatives.

As the service got under way, I was thinking not only of our own grief but also of the pain of all the others who had lost loved ones. I was hoping, too, that we would get through the service in as dignified a manner as we could. On the surface I hope that we appeared calm and collected, but inside we were churning. There was so much to think about, so much had happened, and there was so much to face in the future. But, with God's help, we could only take one step at a time.

The words and the music of the funeral service gave me strength. It is at such a time of deep loss that I feel so strongly the presence and help of God. I know that some people are not believers and that they cannot find such strength, though they desperately need help. I feel so sorry for them. I do not know how I would cope if I did not have a deep faith in God and in His protective care.

My feelings were captured beautifully in the New Testament reading from the reassuring words of Romans 8: 'For I am convinced that neither death nor life, neither angels or demons, neither the present or the future, nor any powers, neither height nor depth, nor anything else in all creation, will be able to separate us from the love of God that is in Christ Jesus our Lord' – and our minister, the Reverend Tom Magowan, added, 'Nor IRA bomb'.

How I clung to those words. I prayed silently, too, for Mr Magowan, who had such a difficult task in leading the service. He had known Marie so well, and I knew that he was deeply moved, not only as a friend of the family, but as a father himself. Marie's uncle, the Reverend Dr Hedley Plunkett, read a portion of Scripture. Sometimes we don't realize what a funeral takes out of the officiating clergy and those who are asked to give an address. Beneath the surface they, too, are dealing with deep emotions, but because they are expressing their sentiments on behalf of all of us, they cannot afford to show their real feelings.

Sometimes, the deepest emotions are beyond words. The first verse of Isaac Watts' great hymn 'I sing the almighty power of God' gave assurance as we left the church, to face the future.

> I sing the almighty power of God
> That made the mountains rise,
> That spread the flowing seas abroad
> And built the lofty skies.

On the way down the aisle, the Bishop of Clogher, the Right Reverend Brian Hannon, reached out and touched my arm. He whispered, 'Well done.' That gave me strength, and I appreciated his kind gesture. Sometimes you or I can do a great deal with just a touch that goes beyond words. Gordon used to remark, at funerals or at other times of need, 'A handshake says it all.'

We needed God's grace for the future. We had chosen Charles Wesley's 'Love Divine, all loves excelling' as the last hymn. It was a favourite which we had sung at our wedding. Now it was being sung at our daughter's funeral, and I felt that it somehow related to Marie's last words of love to her father as they both lay in the dusk and darkness of the rubble, in the midst of pain and of utter chaos, especially this verse,

> Come, Almighty to deliver,
> Let us all Thy grace receive;
> Suddenly return, and never,
> Never more Thy temples leave.
> Thee we would be always blessing,
> Serve Thee as Thy hosts above,
> Pray, and praise Thee without ceasing,
> Glory in Thy perfect love.

We moved out of the church and back into the glare of the cameras outside. People were kind and supportive, and the service, though very emotional and difficult, had not been as big an ordeal as I had feared. By the grace of God we had been given the strength to get through it.

On our way to the cemetery, we passed the Presbyterian Church where the funeral service for Edward Armstrong, another victim of the bomb, was taking place. It was a grim reminder of the pain which all the others were suffering. At the end of a long and very painful day, we laid Marie to rest, and slowly made our way home with heavy hearts.

Messages of Comfort

Over the next days, weeks and months, a great many flowers, letters, phone calls, and messages of sympathy poured in. They came from all over Ireland, from North and South, and from many other parts of the British Isles and further afield.

We were very moved indeed to receive such messages, particularly as many people had taken great trouble to pour out their hearts to us on paper. This taught me a lesson, because I know what comfort such words can bring. Now when I hear of someone who is bereaved, I write a letter expressing my sympathy and sorrow, and trying to share my own experience. Perhaps this is something you might consider. I know that the personal pain is unbearable, but in the very act of sharing pain you not only help to bring healing to them, but also to yourself.

We received so many fine letters, and it took us weeks to sort them out and to read them properly. In the initial stages one or two stood out. They included a letter from a doctor who had ministered to Marie in the operating theatre of the Erne Hospital. He addressed his letter to Gordon. The words gave me an insight into all that had taken place in trying to save Marie's life, from the time she reached the theatre until we spent the last moments with her as her life was ebbing away in the intensive care room. Neither we, nor Marie, had been alone in those agonizing hours while she fought for her life. Others had fought for her, too, and the knowledge of their dedication brought us much comfort.

Dear Mr Wilson,

Having just got back from Marie's funeral, I am writing to you with a sense of self sorrow. Even though I never knew her, I have been unable to watch news reports about the outrage in our town without being overcome by grief when I think of Marie and about how I struggled, hoped and prayed that she would survive. I myself have a baby daughter – I believe you saw her a few weeks ago when my wife was in your shop. Yesterday evening when I stood the child on my lap and felt so proud of her in her beauty and innocence, I could not help but think of how you must have done the same when your own Marie was a baby. That is why I am writing to you now, as one father to another that I might in this way share in your grief.

I don't know if you are aware that when Marie was brought into hospital on Sunday her heart had already stopped. It was promptly restarted by the doctors in Casualty and she was then transferred to the Intensive Care Unit. I arrived there soon afterwards, having learned about the tragedy on my way to church. It became apparent that Marie was bleeding internally so we moved her to theatre where three surgeons worked heroically to bring the bleeding under control. The team of nurses and theatre assistants, most of whom were there voluntarily, were marvellous in the support they gave to the surgeons and to myself. The laboratory staff rendered me an incredible service, performing vital blood tests and letting me know the results very quickly, and supplying me with as much blood as I wanted. The hospital blood stocks ran out eventually, but more soon arrived from Omagh so that at no time were we unable to carry on with the transfusion.

Towards the end of the operation it became obvious that Marie's brain had died even though her heart was still beating. After taking her back up to Intensive Care I felt profoundly heart-broken when I had to tell your wife that we held no hope for Marie at all.

Over the years, of course, I have lost other critically ill patients and although I have always felt saddened on such occasions, I can truly say that I have never been as distressed by the death of a patient as I was when I lost Marie.

I was very moved to see you on television and to hear the words you spoke despite the fact that what you have experienced was horrific beyond belief. I admire your courage and your truly Christian attitude to those who had so cruelly taken the life of your daughter whom you obviously loved so much. I just thank God that you were given the grace to say what you did, and that the sentiments you expressed have gone around the whole world.

I particularly remember one other letter, from a nurse in the Royal Belfast Hospital for Sick Children. She was also the mother of a nurse, and she had written a poem in memory of Marie. She said in her letter:

I hope that I am not intruding upon your sorrow. I never knew Marie, but have written this little poem about her. I would like it to be a comfort to you.

Your love and dignity have impressed us all, and were a glorious witness of your faith. If I have offended, please forgive me – I offer these words to you in love. Please destroy them if you wish. Thank you for showing such love and grace in your sorrow.

Of course we were not offended. On the contrary, we found the letter and the poem most moving and touching, and they helped us. We replied to the nurse who had written to us, expressing our thanks. So, don't be afraid to write to someone in need and to offer kindness and support. Believe me, it will be appreciated.

The Struggle to Forgive

People have often said to me, 'I was very impressed by the way in which you forgave the people who killed your daughter', but it wasn't as easy as that. They said the same to Gordon, although he did not actually use the word 'forgiveness' in his first statement to the media. He said, 'I bear no ill-will'. This is something with which he struggled for a long time. He believed that the bombers' crime was so heinous that only God could forgive them, provided that they would have a change of heart and repent. I know that he also wrestled, as I did, with that passage from the Lord's Prayer which states, 'Forgive us our trespasses as we forgive them that trespass against us.'

In time, Gordon did forgive them in his own way, and I know that he prayed for them every night, as I do. But even his forgiveness got him into trouble with some people. They scorned him and said, 'What right have you to forgive these people?' The philosophy of 'an eye for an eye' was still in their minds and hearts. In the end Gordon made his peace with God and with His forgiveness, but in human terms it was not easy.

It was not easy for me either. My initial reaction to the bombers was one of sustained rage and anger. I was in no mood to even consider 'turning the other cheek'. These dastardly people had planted and detonated explosives which had killed and maimed innocent people and plunged so many families, and the entire community, into grief and despair. And for what? What cause could possibly justify such murderous brutality?

Some people no doubt misunderstood what appeared to be

our initial reaction. Some of them could not believe that we could be so forgiving, but they did not know the whole story. My mind was in continual turmoil. I tried to pray about forgiveness, but for days, weeks and months I wrestled with bitter anger. I understand fully the thoughts of those who feel that they simply cannot forgive. For each of us it is a hard choice, to go on resenting or in the end to be eaten up by our own anger.

I thought of all the victims and I thought specially of Marie, and of her beauty, her innocence, her youth and her love. And I also thought of those who had killed her, hiding up somewhere, not admitting their guilt to friends or family, perhaps even being afraid of admitting their guilt to themselves. I asked myself in the darkness of sleepless nights and in the grey light of a new day what kind of people they were. Did they have families of their own, how could they face their wives, children and parents, knowing what they had done, was there no spark of conscience deep in their violent nature which would make them reflect, even for a moment, on the blood they had shed, on the suffering and pain they had caused? Again and again I asked myself, 'How could they set a bomb to kill so many innocent people? How could they live with themselves?' But there was no simple answer.

However, as I tortured myself with these questions, I was also aware that this was hurting me more than it was hurting them. I was clear that if I did not resolve this in the depths of my being, I too would become a victim of their violence in a different way, apart from being a mother who was grieving for her child. I knew that if I allowed this anger to enter my soul they would eat into me and in the end consume me. I knew that I desperately needed help. All my life I had been trained to ask for God's help, and in the depths of my bitterness, anger and despair, I did so again.

I knew, however, that if I turned to God I would have to be sincere. There was no point in praying one thing, and thinking and acting another. I searched the Scriptures for help, and I pondered on verses 14 and 15 from the 6th chapter of Matthew's Gospel: 'For if you forgive men when they sin against you, your heavenly Father will also forgive you. But if you do not forgive men their sins, your Father will not forgive your sins.' I also thought of the words of Christ on the Cross, 'Father, forgive them, for they do not know what they are doing.'

There was no getting away from that challenge. The message was stark and clear. Slowly and painfully I turned my thoughts and prayers towards forgiveness. I would like to say that this came immediately and easily, but it didn't. My sense of forgiveness came gradually, and in time the anger and bitterness left me. I still have an empty feeling, and I would still like to see the bombers brought to justice.

At times I still think of them – what are they doing now, what are their families like, will their guilt get the better of them as they grow older? Most of all I am more at peace with myself, now that the cold anger has drained away. If you are gripped in anger and bitterness, I understand your feelings. It is very human to think that way, but I hope that you can find your path through to the beginning of a sense of forgiveness. In the end anger and bitterness only add to your pain. When I think now of the people who killed Marie, I have no bitterness remaining. I leave them in the hands of God.

The Empty Place

One of the great difficulties of trying to come to terms with bereavement is the familiarity of everyday things which you associate with the beloved person who is no longer there – an empty place at the table, a snatch of a tune which reminds you of them, their favourite colour, an old school satchel in the roof-space, a battered pair of glasses, even the smell of a garden which they loved.

It is particularly difficult also to explain death to very small children, or at least I thought it would be. On her first visit to the family home after Marie's death, my eldest grand-daughter Eloise, who was then four, ran up the stairs. She entered Marie's bedroom and called out, 'Granny, where has Marie gone, I want her back!'

I was astounded, and in my weak state of body and mind I was not prepared for such a searching question. So I shot an arrow prayer to God and said, 'Please help me to answer this little child truthfully.'

I kneeled down and drew her to me and quietly said, 'Eloise, Marie has gone away to God's house, we cannot bring her back to be with us again, you and I have to travel a long journey to her.' To my great relief she accepted my explanation. She ran off to play, leaving me shattered and realizing how this little child was herself grieving and missing a much-loved aunt who had also loved her so deeply.

I recalled the words of David after the death of his son: 'Can I bring him back again? I will go to him, but he will not return to me.' The best way to travel that lonesome journey is with God as our guide. We missed Marie terribly, but we found great solace in a poem whose origin I am uncertain of but it was sent to us, I recall, by a parent who also had lost a child.

To Any Parent

Say not the girl is dead, but rather say
She's but a little further on the way,
Impatient sooner to behold the view –
At the next turning you may see it too.
Say she's a child again, early to bed
On night's soft pillow fain to lay her head.
Say, she is off to track the mountain stream
And lingers by the side in girlish dream.
Say, by immortal waters now at rest,
She clasps a thousand memories to her breast.
Say to her wondering quests, wise angels smiling
Tell the true story of the world's beguiling.
Say on heroic task her soul is thrilling
Where noble dream hath noble deed fulfilling.
Say to high festival she moves in state
Enfranchised, aureolic, immaculate.
Say that she feasts with comrades tried and true
But in her heart the banquet waits for you.
Say, in the Presence, at a gentle word
She shows the wound marks to her wounded Lord.
Say NEVER she is dead, but rather say
She's but a little further on the way.

No Longer Strangers

When Marie died, it was not just our circle of friends and acquaintances who supported us so much. Letters and messages poured in from people we had never met – all kinds of people from home and overseas. All of these brought great comfort, and we were amazed at how often the words of total strangers would chime with our own thoughts. Anyone who is suffering greatly hopes that in some way good will emerge out of the tragedy or wrong they are experiencing.

The kindness of strangers and the comfort their words so often bring are surely one way in which this happens. It was particularly helpful to realize that people had gone to great trouble to share their sympathy with us, often from the other side of the world – as in this letter posted from Australia:

Dear Gordon and Joan,

My wife and I have grieved for you in the course of the terrible days since Remembrance Sunday. Our hearts go out to you in your anguish, and we pray earnestly that the Lord will sustain you in your suffering.

If it is of any consolation to you at all, there is a great well of sympathy for you here. Gordon's voice has been heard on numerous occasions, and you have been seen on national television. Your spirit of Christian forgiveness, your heart-rending narrative and your character-istic courage have all made a deep impression in the Australian community.

I would say that, more than any other factor, your moving testimony has stamped the name of Enniskillen on the hearts of the people here. There has been more attention to the Ulster situation in one tragic week than in the previous five years put together. We also perceive that, out of the suffering of an entire community, and particularly of heroic individuals like yourselves, a new understanding has developed, and the nature and depth of the suffering of good, decent, Christian people have been more clearly grasped.

As it happened, I was away from home on a Management Course last week. I was, however, able to call my wife and comfort her each evening. Her distress was very real, and she shed many tears on your account. We have both been praying much for you, and we shall continue to commend you to the love and the compassion of our God.

Sometimes the letters we so simple and beautiful that they brought tears to our eyes, as in this letter from a little girl in Bristol:

Dear Mr Wilson

When I heard your daughter was killed in the Enniskillen bombing I was very upset. From the pictures in the paper your daughter was a lovely girl. She was very pretty and I'm sure she was a super nurse. I am eight years old and I do hope I grow up like Marie. I am so sorry, there are people who do such horrid things. Please don't be sad about Marie. I am sure she is so happy in Heaven, I will never forget her.

Love
Katy
XXXX

Through the Eyes of Others

Sometimes we think that we knew almost everything about our beloved one who has departed, but I found that the letters and tributes from Marie's friends and colleagues provided a new dimension to her life and work. She was our daughter, but she was also a young, professional woman who was making her way in life, and other people's views about Marie brought us such comfort. Perhaps you are finding this also, in the midst of your bereavement.

One of the finest tributes came from George Young who was then Headmaster of Enniskillen Collegiate, Marie's old school. George was also our neighbour and our friend. He wrote in the school magazine:

> The death of Marie Wilson in the bomb explosion on Remembrance Sunday brought a deep sadness to all of us in school who knew her. The response of her family, characterized by their decision that the service on the day of her funeral should be one of thanksgiving for her life rather than one of mourning for her death, is a fitting lead for us all in this school community in our reaction.
>
> While she was here with us Marie was the embodiment of integrity, goodwill, enthusiasm, a warm regard for everyone and a brisk no-nonsense cheerfulness. Self-pity played no part in her make up and her example ensured that those around her did not succumb to it either.
>
> Whatever she did – and she was willing to tackle

everything – was always given her total and best efforts and like Oliver Goldsmith she touched nothing she did not adorn.

We are all the poorer for her passing, but we are grateful for what she gave us and for the memories she has left behind.

One very special letter, which meant so much to us, gave a picture of Marie's last working day at the Children's Hospital in Belfast. It came from Marie M. Donald, an auxiliary nurse. She wrote:

I worked with Marie Wilson in the Royal Belfast Hospital for Sick Children during the last two weeks of her life and I have never, in fifteen years as a nursing auxiliary, been so drawn to anyone.

She was the most delightful girl, with all the qualities required by a good nurse. As the days passed, I was struck by her caring and her compassion which she had in abundance. I once saw her eyes fill with tears whilst nursing a mentally handicapped child, and the gentle way she handled the sick babies was very moving.

Her spontaneous friendliness was very infectious. She greeted everyone with that lovely smile, and they responded in like manner.

We had a lot of things in common, for two people of different age, we both sang in a choir, we liked the same music, she was the same age as my daughter and, another little bond, we shared the same Christian name.

On the day she was leaving our ward, I spoke to her for the last time, and my words comfort me now. I am so pleased I said them to her when she was alive and not about her when she was dead. I told her she had the most beautiful disposition and that her mother and father could be very proud of her. I also said if ever I was ill it would be lovely to be cared for by her.

As she left the ward I wished her good luck in the future. Three days later she was dead. When I saw her father on television I knew that only such a man as he could have a daughter like her.

It was my privilege to know Marie for that short time and I will never forget her. Nurse Marie Wilson was special and I am sure God thought so too.

It also helped us that the League of Nurses paid tribute to Marie in their journal. Sister Florence Betty wrote:

Nursing was her first love. She enjoyed caring for sick people, quietly and unobtrusively giving of her best to ensure their comfort. She also sang in the hospital choir and played the violin. Marie was a winsome, happy girl who endeared herself to all those who knew her and worked with her.

Many of her nursing friends and companions joined in the service of thanksgiving for her life, held in Darling Street Methodist Church, Enniskillen on Tuesday 10th November 1987. The church was filled and overflowing with sorrowing people, but the atmosphere was triumphant, as the words of Isaac Watts' great hymn resounded through the building:

> God's hand is my perpetual guard,
> He guides me with His eye.
> Why should I then forget the Lord,
> Whose love is ever nigh?

These are words of assurance, hope and comfort.

Marie Wilson was the first of our student nurses to pay the supreme sacrifice. She will be remembered as a gallant, dedicated and loyal colleague.

Angel Voice

Five days after Marie's death, I was trying to concentrate on reading my daily portion from the Bible, and Scripture Union notes. I was greatly helped and encouraged by verses 12 and 13 from 1 Peter, chapter 4. These words were a beacon of light in my deep, deep grieving:

> Beloved, think it not strange concerning the fiery trial which is to try you, as though some strange thing happened unto you: but rejoice, inasmuch as ye are partakers of Christ's sufferings; that, when His glory shall be revealed, ye may be glad also with exceeding joy.

As I read this passage, I felt that the Lord Jesus was so near. Some weeks later, I was having a very down day. I was very sad, distressed and depressed, feeling that I would never get over Marie's death. I wandered into her bedroom, and on her empty bed lay many books which thoughtful people had sent to help us. At random I picked up a publication entitled *Be Still My Soul* [2] and I noticed that it was signed by the author: 'With deepest sympathy from Elizabeth Urch'.

I began reading her book, and I was gripped by its contents. Elizabeth had experienced great grief and heartache when her beloved young husband, the Reverend Walter Urch, had died. In the book she included a sermon which her husband had preached a short time before his death, and it was based on those verses from 1 Peter which had meant so much to me over the previous weeks.

The sermon was so powerful, beautiful and helpful that it set me on to a higher plane, and the entire book has been read and re-read, over the years. I came to know Elizabeth Urch personally, and to cherish her wisdom as well as her warm and sincere friendship. I continually appreciate her deep spiritual insights and lovely infectious humour, and I thank God for her. God has used her book to soothe many suffering people.

Keeping in Contact

I have learned many lessons from the people who write at the time of bereavement. Many of them have amazed me by the way in which they continue caring, writing and keeping in touch as the years go by.

One day I had a lovely surprise visit from a young man, Stephen Morris. His grandparents in Yorkshire, Mr and Mrs Hinchcliffe, had written to us when Marie died. Each year they kept in touch with Christmas, Easter and anniversary cards.

When they passed on, their daughter Mrs Margaret Morris wrote telling us the sad news, but the connection was maintained. When Margaret knew that her son Stephen, a violinist in the Medici String Quartet, was giving a concert in Enniskillen, she asked him to call on us. We spent about an hour talking to Stephen and heard so much about his grandparents and their strong Christian faith. I was so thrilled to meet him, and his visit made my day. The concert that evening was very special too. He asked me to remember him and his musical career in my prayers, and I do.

There were a number of other lovely people who kept in touch, including Eyrl and Bethan Edwards from Bala in North Wales. They wrote to us after the bomb. Eyrl's Sunday School class sent a card, signed by all the children. They visited us twice in Enniskillen, and Eyrl phoned monthly. He also sent us tapes of Welsh choirs.

Agnes Dignan from Dublin visited Enniskillen each November with flowers for the Cenotaph, and she sent us Christmas,

Easter and Remembrance Day messages annually. Martina Waite, a Belfast woman whom Marie had nursed in the Royal Victoria Hospital, still battles with ill-health but she sends me lovely letters and helpful tapes. She has a great sense of humour which keeps me humble and protects me from self-pity.

We also received lovely messages from those who had experienced the loss of young ones, including John Donlon from Warrington, whose nephew Jonathan Ball died when Provisional IRA bombs exploded in a crowded shopping precinct in the town on 20 March 1993; and Colin and Wendy Parry, whose son Timothy also died in the explosions. John, Colin and Wendy have kept in touch regularly, and I greatly value their friendship. The Mayor of Warrington also sends an annual Christmas card.

Elsie Cowley from Edwinstone writes every November, Christmas and Easter, and she has shown great love and understanding. Her daughter was killed in a motor accident by a drunken driver. She has kept in touch all the way through since Marie's death, and Peter and Gordon's passing.

All these people have brought great comfort, not least becuse they have stayed in touch. Maybe you also have regular contact with people who sympathized with you in your bereavement. All these contacts with such special people are a reminder that perhaps we, too, should stay in touch with others to whom we have written in their hour of need.

Christmas

One of the most difficult times of all was our first Christmas, particularly as it came so soon after Marie's death. Christmas was always for us a time of celebration, with family reunions, and a sense of love, cheer and warmth amid 'the bleak mid-winter'. It was so different that year. Marie's death hung over everything like a dark cloud that threatened to crowd out all the hope and rejoicing of the special Christmas season. The memories of that first Christmas after Marie's death never fade.

Despite some beautiful, passing moments, we were relieved when the festive season was over. We went through it in a state of exhaustion, and I wanted to get back to the routine of daily life. The memories were too painful. It was a sad, sad, Christmas without Marie.

In the run-up to Christmas there were many cards, messages and flowers from all kinds of people. I struggled through a little children's orchestra performance for parents. The children were most supportive and tried to play their very best as we went through the range of carols. The Methodist Church choir's carol service was uplifting, and I accompanied them to the Erne Hospital.

We actually sang in the Intensive Care Ward where Marie had died. I found that extremely difficult, but I felt it was something I had to do. I conducted the choir, swallowed hard, and concentrated on the great words from the carol by Mrs Alexander: 'Once in royal David's city':

And our eyes at last shall see him,
Through his own redeeming love;
For that Child so dear and gentle
Is our Lord in heaven above;
And he leads his children on
To the place where he is gone.

Not in that poor lowly stable,
With the oxen standing by,
We shall see him, but in heaven,
Set at God's right hand on high,
When, like stars, his children crowned
All in white shall wait around.

We spent Christmas Day with Ingrid and Peter who did their best to lift our spirits. Our two grand-daughters, with their joy in Santa's presents, provided healing therapy. As I watched them play with their toys, the words of the popular carol came to mind:

Girls and boys leave your toys, make no noise,
Kneel at His crib and worship Him,
For this shrine, Child Divine,
Is the sign our Saviour's here.
Alleluia, the church bells ring
Alleluia, the angels sing
Alleluia from everything, all must draw near.[3]

Unexpected Moments of Happiness

I find comfort every year in the traditional images of Christmas. I received a Christmas card from Ruth Fullerton, a family friend, who wrote a poem which brought home to me the simple yet profound message of Christmas.

There is no doubt that it can be a most difficult time for families, and especially for those who mourn, but somehow if you can allow your mind and spirit to search for the essential message of Christmas – God coming into the world to bear its sorrow and sin and to give us new life – eventually its reassurance, warmth and joy will help to take away some of the chill that can threaten to freeze your very heart. In the midst of my grief, this little poem by Ruth reminded me of the fleeting happiness which I had experienced earlier while accompanying our church choir in the Carol Service before Christmas.

> Lovely winter evening
> Frost and snow around
> I can hear bells pealing
> What a joyful sound
> Calling me to worship
> Jesus, God's dear son
> Born in Bethlehem's stable
> Precious little one
> I shall join in singing
> Carols old and new
> Gather with the faithful

> Though we may be few
> Then I'll journey homeward,
> Tramping through the snow
> Thinking of the Baby
> Born so long ago

Cherish such moments and hold on to the memories of them; they are signs that hope will return. Why not keep a note of them so that you can remind yourself of the fleeting happiness when hope seems to be very far away?

Gordon's Illness

Just when you have experienced little shafts of light in the gloom, the darkness crowds in again. Gordon had not been terribly well in the weeks after the bomb. He had been injured in the blast, and he had been in great pain. As well as that there was the emotional trauma of trying to cope with Marie's death, as well as the attendant publicity, and the attention from the media.

Early in the New Year he suffered a collapse and a complete loss of memory. It was a most worrying time for all of us. He had begun to talk total nonsense. He asked me, 'When is Marie coming home?' That shook me, and I immediately called the doctor. When he arrived Gordon asked, 'Who is this stranger?'

Gordon was sent immediately to the Erne Hospital for observation. He was in a confused state for maybe 16 to 24 hours, but then he recovered, and behaved as normal. However, we were all on our guard, and he was sent to the Royal Victoria Hospital in Belfast for further tests.

I found it difficult to accompany him, as I dreaded seeing the young nurses in uniform, because I knew that they would remind me of Marie. I prayed to God to give me strength, and as I arrived at the hospital, a sense of peace flowed over me. I thanked God for such a place of healing. Many of Marie's young nursing friends came to see us, and brought us comfort and cheer.

Looking back on my sense of dread, I am so glad that peace and comfort came out of what might have been such an ordeal. I am convinced that my prayers were answered, and this experience reminds me of the wonderful hymn by Joseph Scriven:

> What a friend we have in Jesus
> All our sins and grief to bear!
> What a privilege to carry
> Everything to God in prayer!

When Gordon had recovered sufficiently to allow him to travel, we all took a much-needed holiday in the Caribbean. We were totally exhausted by the journey, but we found healing in the sun and the sea. I met a widow who told me about her bereavement and how the waves of grief would sweep over her and then recede. Gradually, she said, there would be longer periods between each bout of grief. And so it proved.

I never forgot her kind words and the help she brought me. I also found great solace in the company of Julie-Anne, whose love and care were a great help to us. All too soon the holiday was over and we had to return home to pick up the pieces.

The First Snowdrops

During the first awful weeks after Marie's death, I found that long walks were very therapeutic. There is something about walking in the countryside or a park and about Nature's cycles of birth, death and re-birth which speak to your heart. There is a reassurance that after the long winter, new growth springs from the ground, just as the first buds of recovery and of hope begin to appear from your own dark winter of suffering and sorrow.

I recall particularly one walk in the lovely grounds of Castle-coole, a large National Trust property on the outskirts of Enniskillen. The muted colours of winter were all around but as I turned a corner, I saw a bank of snowdrops ahead of me and I suddenly burst into tears. All alone, I roared and cried and shook with great sobs. I thought I was going totally out of control.

I hoped that no-one was around, as I could not stop sobbing. Eventually the tears subsided, but I still shuddered and sighed. As I walked on, I realized that this outburst had somehow released me, and that the sight of the snowdrops had unleashed an emotional dam inside me. The lines from Handel's Messiah came to me, 'A man of sorrows and acquainted with grief'. I felt again that God was with me, sharing my grief, healing me and somehow bringing me through.

The little snowdrops, so vulnerable yet so sturdy, had taught me a lesson about hope and survival in the midst of a deep winter of personal suffering. I thought, too, of the story about the snowdrop which, in the winter sunshine, draws some of the warmth in its petals, and then at night-time it closes the petals and holds that warmth to itself. This is a bit like grieving. In the midst of the sorrow, you find words of encouragement and hope which you draw around yourself for comfort during the dark nights of the soul which inevitably come to you in the midst of your grief.

I have always been fond of snowdrops, which to me are always a miracle of beauty and sturdiness, and a symbol of new growth and of hope.

> The virgin snowdrop like a lambent fire
> Pierces the cold earth with its green streaked spire . . .

> Hartley Coleridge

Later on, I realized that the walk at Castlecoole, and the sight of the first snowdrops, had been a turning point in my grieving. After so many weeks of bearing up as best I could, and of trying to give support to Gordon and to my children and their families, I had let go and did not try to stop the flow of tears. Some people call this 'the big cry', and it often happens at an unexpected moment, triggered by something quite small even. It seems unendurable while it lasts, but tears need to flow.

So, if you feel like crying, go ahead. Even if you are a man. In our Western society people sometimes say 'Grown men don't cry', but they do. I heard Gordon sob, behind closed doors, and I did not try to stop him. I knew that this was his way of trying to come to terms with what had happened. In my own way, I also experienced healing from my sobbing.

> Lord take these tears, mortality's relief,
> and till we share your joys forgive our grief.

> Alexander Pope

Mothers' Day

❦

The pain of Mothers' Day, especially the first after a child's death, is terrible. One misses the smile, the outstretched arms, the hugs and kisses, and the warm greeting – 'Happy Mothers' Day!'

My last Mothers' Day present from Marie, chosen as ever with care and presented with her big-hearted exuberance, was a coffee mug with the inscription: 'Mum – 24 hours working woman – pie baker, bed maker, socks finder, clock winder, clothes mender, money lender, grocery-shopper, argument stopper, organiser, economiser, laundry-doer, health renewer, room inspector, social director, child-guider, hug provider'.

That inscription on the mug said it all, and I was only too grateful to have been all those things to Marie, to Peter and Julie-Anne. I was, and am, grateful to have such an everyday reminder of Marie's love and affection. Perhaps you, too, find solace in the everyday objects which your loved one once used, or gave to you – a favourite book, a vase, a travel bag, a key-ring, even a mug.

Somehow the fact that they handled such ordinary things brings them back to you in a most extraordinary way. Each Mothers' Day I take down the mug which Marie gave to me, and I re-read the 'mother's task' with a sad smile. No matter how much you put a brave face on things, you will always miss them. This was brought home to me by the words of a radio broadcast, the author of which, unfortunately, I have not been able to trace. But I thank the speaker who so beautifully summarized my feelings, and perhaps yours too:

Nothing affects our lives like the death of a child, nothing unnerves us like the death of a child, nothing can fill the gap, there is the gap of communication on our mind every day. She stretches out to hold me, a part of her, a part of me is there. Is she truly yet with me and I with her?

In a strange way, my Mothers' Day mug still brings Marie and me together. Do you also have a special present from your loved one which you will never forget? If so, treasure it, for it is a gift beyond price and beyond compare.

The First Easter

Easter is a particularly poignant time for those who are bereaved, but there is great hope and reassurance in the Resurrection, with the triumphant message

> Christ is risen!
> He is risen indeed!

On the first Easter after Marie's death, I visited her grave in Enniskillen Cemetery early on Easter Sunday morning. It was absolutely still, with no-one about. I placed a bunch of daffodils from our own garden on her grave, and while I stood there quietly reflecting on the terrible events of the previous few months, I thought of Marie's life and death, and of the uplifting and comforting story of the Resurrection of Christ, from Luke chapter 24:

> On the first day of the week, very early in the morning, the women took the spices they had prepared and went to the tomb. They found the stone rolled away from the tomb, but when they entered they did not find the body of the Lord Jesus. While they were wondering about this, suddenly two men in clothes that gleamed like lightning stood beside them. In their fright the women bowed down with their faces to the ground, but the men said to them, 'Why do you look for the living among the dead? He is not here; he has risen! Remember how he told you, while he was still with you in Galilee: The Son

of Man must be delivered into the hands of sinful men,
be crucified and on the third day be raised again.' Then
they remembered his words.

These words are of great reassurance to anyone who has lost a
loved one. They were of comfort to me on that Easter morning
when I stood by Marie's grave, and they still give me strength.
I am aware that many people may not be able to share the
comfort of these words, no matter how hard they try to do so,
but I hope that by quiet searching their souls will find solace
from their suffering, and hope for the future. I have known
people with no discernible religious faith who really want to
believe in the possibility of a life beyond the grave, where they
will once again be united with those whom they loved.

The reality of death faces us all, but it is a great inspiration
to read words like those of Abbé de Tourville:

Life limited by death? Nonsense. That is a great mistake.
Death hardly counts. We already have eternal life, and
that should give us great tranquillity, as those who feel
themselves to be eternal. Do not therefore be afraid of
death. It is the flowering of life, the consummation of
union with God.[4]

Easter, with its central message of suffering, death and resurrection, is a time for deep reflection and meditation, especially
after the death of a loved one. It is also a time which fills us
with reassurance and gives us another opportunity to praise
God and to give thanks for the sacrifice and example of Jesus
Christ, the Lord of Lords.

Forever Twenty

Coming of age is one of the happy signs of growing maturity in a young person's life. Though this is now eighteen, tradition-ally it was associated with the twenty-first birthday, when the young man or woman was given 'the key of the house', as we say in Enniskillen. This was to symbolize the fact that a son or daughter was old enough to make his or her own decisions, and could come and go in the house as they pleased – though I remember that my own parents still had a lot to say about my comings and goings, long after I was twenty-one!

Marie, who died when she was only twenty, would have come of age on 29 April, and as the day approached I could not help thinking of what it would have meant to us. Probably we would have had a big party, with all the family and relatives present, with a cake, birthday cards and presents. I am sure that Gordon would have made a speech, and that Marie would have teased him, as she always did.

It is only human for a parent to think of these things, even if you know that such things cannot possibly be. However, there is some consolation in memory, in the mind-picture of your young one looking strong, vivacious and vibrant. I thought of Marie in that way too, and my vision of her was summed up so wonderfully by John Masefield in his poem 'Beauty':

I have seen dawn and sunset and windy hills
Coming in solemn beauty like slow old tunes of Spain;

I have seen the lady April bringing the daffodils
Bringing the springing grass and soft warm April rain.

I have heard the song of blossom and the old chant of the
  sea
And seen strange lands from under the arched white sails
  of ships,
But the loveliest things of beauty God ever has showed to
  me
  Are her voice, and her hair, and the dear red curve of
  her lips.[5]

On the evening after Marie's death, one of my best friends
came to see me, and I shall never forget her words, which were
so different and so sincere. She took my hand and said simply
and directly, 'Well, Joan, Marie will be always twenty.'

I have clung to those words and cherished them. I tell her
frequently how much they meant then, and still mean to me.
It helps me to recall the youthful Marie and her lovely smile.
To me she will always be twenty.

Losing a child is the hardest of all griefs, but in our minds
they will always be young, vibrant and full of promise.

A Voice That Still Speaks

As time passed by, I worried if I would forget the sound of Marie's voice, but I still hear her cheery greeting to everybody, 'Hello and how are you?'

Over the months and years since Marie's death, I have been conscious that many people have died in the Troubles in Northern Ireland, and that although there has been a great deal of talk and comment about the victims of violence, it is these people who no longer have a voice of their own.

In the story of what happened to Marie, the only person who cannot speak is Marie herself. I wonder what she would say today, if we could hear her voice? I am aware, however, that in another sense her voice is still with us through her writings. During her short life, she kept a notebook, and her jottings give us a poignant picture of what she had been thinking.

I know that during her time at the Royal Victoria Hospital she wrestled with many doubts. Gordon and I read and re-read one note she left, and she called it 'My prayer, after studying the Epistle of James'. She had been reading chapter 4, verses 13–16:

> Go to now, ye that say, To day or to morrow we will go into such a city, and continue there a year, and buy and sell, and get gain: whereas ye know not what shall be on the morrow. For what is your life? It is even a vapour, that appeareth for a little time, and then vanisheth away. For that ye ought to say, If the Lord will, we shall live, and this do, or that.

Marie's notes on the Epistle of James which she had studied in the Crescent Church in Belfast with the Reverend Derick Bingham, gave us a wonderful insight into the life and mind of our beloved daughter. She wrote:

> Thank you, Lord, for your Word. Without you I, too, would be an orphan. Lord help me by bringing others to be blessed, also help me to grow in maturity and completeness, and receive the crown of life.
>
> Lord, my career is up-front in my mind at the moment, with Night Duty. Help me to listen to my patients and act on their problems. Lord, I pray for my great friends, Mum and Dad, thank you for their love. Jaws (her sister) please Lord be with her, and especially Anne-Marie. I pray for Northern Ireland and the whole world. I pray for the church that I may do my role. Thank you Lord, give me wisdom.

I think it is fitting that Marie has the last word here. Maybe your loved one has left a letter or a tape-recording or video message which you can read or watch, and this might bring you comfort. In a strange way it helps to keep them alive in your hearts and your thoughts, where they will always remain fresh and unblemished. That is a great comfort.

Unhappy Anniversary

Anniversaries play a great part in our lives: anniversaries and other milestones that we remember, or which we *ought* to have remembered!

In Ireland we also remember other anniversaries, almost to excess. Our calendar is full of commemoration ceremonies for events in our history which are perhaps best forgotten. The only point in remembering the past is to try to learn from it, something which we in Ireland – North and South – are tragically slow in picking up.

It is family anniversaries, however, which are best remembered. As the months wore on after Marie's death, I began to dread the anniversary of the Enniskillen bombing. It had been a difficult year for all of us, and not least for Gordon. After all the initial publicity, he seemed to withdraw into himself. He kept replaying the video of the events of that time, to the point where Julie-Anne and I thought it was not right to go on doing that. We tried to help him take his mind off what happened, but for months it was an uphill struggle.

As spring passed into summer, and the autumn approached, I hated the thoughts of the winter and the long nights, and – above all – the approaching anniversary of Marie's death. Make no mistake about it, some anniversaries are not easy, and none is more difficult than the approaching anniversary of the death of a child. It was around this time that I discovered these words by Anna Sewell, the author of *Black Beauty*. They were written following the death of her niece, Little Blossom Johnston.

Seven young trees grew close together,
All fresh and green in the summer weather.
A little one, beautiful, tender and tall
Grew in the middle, the joy of them all
And lovingly turning their branches to-gether
They circled it round in the fine summer weather.
On the Sabbath eve of an autumn day
The beautiful plant was taken away
And left a lonely and leafless space
And nothing was found to fill the place.
Nothing of rich, nothing of rare
Could fill the spot that was left so bare,
Nothing below, nothing above
Could fill this empty spot but love.
Then closer the young trees grew to-gether
In the chilly days of that autumn weather
And every branch put forth a shoot
And new life quickened at the root.
They grew in winter, in spring they grew
Silently nourished by heavenly dew
And when they came back to summer weather
One beautiful group they stood to-gether
And their greenest leaves hung o'er the place
Where the youngest had stood in its tender grace.
Nothing below, nothing above
Nothing can heal the hurt, but LOVE.[6]

This piece appealed to me in the midst of the first autumn after Marie's death, approaching that dreaded first anniversary, and I wrote it down specially to keep and read for comfort – it was so true. Nothing below, nothing above, could fill this gap but love. When you come across a passage which will help you to get through the dark days, I would encourage you to write it down and turn to it in your times of need. This passage, which I read and re-read, certainly helped me.

A Hymn for the Heart

The first anniversary of the bomb that devastated our lives was marked in Enniskillen by a special service in the local Presbyterian Church, which was attended by the families of the bereaved and injured and by their friends, and by those who gave us their love and their prayers. It was a lovely service, and I could feel a great wall of support all around us.

Yet even in the midst of this, I felt *so* down in spirits. I am sure that the other relatives felt just the same as I did. As the service progressed, all the loving words and messages of comfort were of great help, but I remember flicking through the Presbyterian hymn-book, and I found this hymn by John Campbell Sharp, which spoke to my heart. The first two verses in particular captured the turbulent emotions we had all experienced in the previous twelve months, but there was also a reminder of the rock-like strength of God who was with us in the midst of our uncertainty, suffering and pain.

> 'Twixt gleams of joy and clouds of doubt
> Our feelings come and go.
> Our best estate is tossed about
> In ceaseless ebb and flow.
> No mood of feeling, form of thought
> Is constant for a day
> But Thou O Lord, Thou changest not,
> The same thou art alway.

I grasp Thy strength, make it my own;
I lose my hold and then comes down
Darkness and cold unrest.
Let me no more my comfort draw
From my frail hold on Thee,
In this alone rejoice with awe,
Thy mighty grasp of me.

Abiding Memories

A comfort in bereavement are the memories of the loved one who is no longer with us – things they did and said, their expressions, little things we remember from years back. I have found that this is not necessarily a continuous remembering, in the sense that we think of them for long periods at a time. Of course, there are special memories at anniversary times – which can be sad and painful – but some of the happiest memories are those which come to you suddenly, in a dream, in the garden, walking through the countryside, sitting in your familiar armchair, when you are driving, or doing some routine chore.

I have a lovely memory of Marie singing solo the hymn 'It is a thing most wonderful' at a children's service in our Methodist Church. The memory of that performance is so fresh in my mind. Each time I hear this hymn I picture the scene – a little girl only nine years old smiling shyly, yet gaining confidence as she sang. One of my choir members told me that she thought it was a most sincere performance, and there was something particularly sensitive about it.

> It is a thing most wonderful,
> Almost too wonderful to be,
> That God's own Son should come from heaven
> And die to save a child like me.
>
> And yet I know that it is true;
> He chose a poor and humble lot,

And wept, and toiled, and mourned, and died,
For love of those who loved Him not.

I sometimes think about the cross,
And shut my eyes and try to see
The cruel nails and crown of thorns,
And Jesus crucified for me.

But even could I see Him die,
I could but see a little part,
Of that great love, which, like a fire,
Is always burning in His heart.

I cannot tell how He could love
A child so weak and full of sin;
His love must be most wonderful,
If He could die my love to win.

It is most wonderful to know
His love for me so free and sure;
But 'tis more wonderful to see
My love for Him so faint and poor.

And yet I want to love Thee, Lord,
O light the flame within my heart,
And I will love Thee more and more
Until I see Thee as Thou art.

William Walsham How (1823–97)

She was reluctant to sing solo, but the organist Richey Wilson
– who was a friend of our family – persuaded her. She had a
great relationship with him, and felt that she could not refuse
his request! Sadly he died in a car accident some years later. It
was the first bereavement in Marie's life, and she took it badly.

Looking back to the day she sang in our church, how pleased

I am now that she did so. It is these little memories which keep you going in the dark days. You have memories of your own: cling to them because they will give you warmth and joy. However, if you find that these happy memories are not coming, don't worry, and don't try to force them. They will come to you in their own good time.

Retreat and Advance

Sometimes, in the midst of an ordinary day, you will find that a great longing comes over you. It is hard to figure out what this is – perhaps it's a mixture of sadness, a deep yearning for what might have been, and a difficulty to accept what has happened. There are no words to express these longings, and they are very private for each individual, but they need to be attended to in our own individual way.

Even in a close and happy marriage such as Gordon and I had, you cannot always be aware of what your partner is thinking, or how he or she copes with grief in their personal way. We all have different memories and different longings. For me the greatest longing at times was to get away from it all to a place where I could be at peace, to find that part of my mind and soul which was above everyday things, and the all-too-present past.

This sense of longing, for me, is captured beautifully in the seventeenth-century hymn by Henry Vaughan (1621–95):

> My soul, there is a country
> Far beyond the stars,
> Where stands a winged sentry
> All skilful in the wars.
>
> There, above noise and danger,
> Sweet peace sits crowned with smiles,
> And One born in a manger
> Commands the beauteous files.

> He is thy gracious friend,
> And – O my soul, awake! –
> Did in pure love descend
> To die here for thy sake.
>
> If Thou canst get but thither
> There grows the flower of peace,
> The rose that cannot wither,
> Thy fortress, and thy ease.
>
> Leave then thy foolish ranges;
> For none can thee secure
> But One who never changes –
> Thy God, thy life, thy cure.

It is not wrong to wish oneself away to these secret places and they come in a variety of forms. For some, it is the company of friends that they need at such times, for others it is solitude. At such times, try to stop what you are doing and call your friend, or take a few moments in a quiet corner. Think of it not as escaping, but as retreating in order to advance.

People ask me, 'Did you ever reach a point where you got over Marie's death?' The answer is 'No, not ever.' However, after the first year or so, I felt that I had travelled a long way, but it took me at least five years to realize that she was not coming back. By that time I had learned to give her up to God.

Bereavement was not a road I ever wanted to set out on, and there were many times when the difficulties seemed so great that I felt that I could not go on. But there was unexpected help too: the kindness we received, the love of friends, the comforts of faith . . . who knows, we might have gone on and returned to that anonymity we knew before the dreadful events that took Marie and others out of our lives. But this was not to be. A second, devastating blow was about to strike us.

PETER

Peter's Death

On 7 December 1994, Peter Wilson was driving on a dark winter evening to his home at Pubble, near Enniskillen. It had been just another normal day. He had his own business and shop as an interior designer, following the closure of his father's drapers shop some years earlier. Gordon, like his own father, had been an enthusiastic draper, who delighted in keeping abreast with the latest fashions and in notching up record sales.

However, he lost heart after the Enniskillen bomb and sold the business. Peter, who had served his time in the drapery trade, decided to start up on his own. He was not as hard-edged as his father, and he had a softer, creative side with a skill for working with colours and design. It seemed an obvious step, with his parents' help, to move into the world of interior designs. He worked hard, and his natural flair, together with his sensitive approach to his customers, boded well for the future.

His wife Ingrid was a primary school teacher in Enniskillen. They had two young daughters, Eloise and Judith. They were a close-knit, happy family and their rock-solid marriage and domestic life were a particular comfort to Joan and Gordon after the nightmare of Marie's premature death.

It was then seven years since she had died, and although the open wound was still painful, friends of Gordon and Joan could see that – to some extent – they were beginning to put the worst of the past behind them. Gordon, in particular, seemed to be coping well. His role as a Member of the Irish Senate, to which he had been appointed by the Irish Premier Albert Reynolds, and his many media and speaking engagements had given him a new lease of life. As ever, Joan was the rock in the background who supported the entire family.

Suddenly and cruelly, their slow, quiet coping was shattered. As Peter drove home on that cold winter evening, his car inexplicably veered across a busy road and ploughed straight into an oncoming lorry. He was badly injured, and died at the scene shortly afterwards. He was thirty-eight. The Wilsons' nightmare began all over again. Joan and her wider family had to try to pick up the pieces once more as they grappled with the horror of this second bereavement.

Another Nightmare

The loss of Peter after Marie's death was indescribable. I had been making special queen cakes for my two grand-daughters that evening, and I was looking forward to seeing them later. Their infectious enthusiasm always lifted my spirits. This was only a month after the anniversary of Marie's death on 8 November, and I was feeling low.

Then the phone rang and Ingrid, my daughter-in-law, told me the dreadful news. She said that Peter had had an accident, that he was under a lorry and was badly hurt. An icy dread gripped my heart. My mind went blank. I only remember throwing down the phone and screaming, as I tried to throw off the reality of what those words meant. I ran screaming upstairs, downstairs, along the corridor and back past the phone. It was off the hook, but I phoned Ingrid again, hoping that it was not true. Herself in shock, she told me again what had happened, but I could not take it in.

I phoned Gordon, who was away at meetings of the Irish Senate, at his hotel in Dublin. He tried to take it calmly and said, 'Find out as much as you can, and ring me back.' Then our minister and his wife arrived. I knew by their faces to expect the worst. They drove me to Ingrid's house, a scene of utter desolation inside and out. I looked at the little girls and their mother, and a wave of despair swept over me. What were we all going to do? There was sleet and snow swirling around the house and drifting between the bare trees. I asked Ingrid point blank, 'Is Peter dead?' With difficulty she replied, 'Granny, I'm afraid so.' I felt all my strength drain away.

I phoned Gordon and told him that Peter had died. He was paralysed with shock, and all he could say was, 'I'll be home.' Somehow he made that long journey back from Dublin in the darkness, with the help of friends, and he arrived in Peter and Ingrid's house just before midnight. He was haggard, and completely numbed with shock. To my dying day I will never forget what he said: 'Joan, this is some loss we have sustained now.' In times of crisis Gordon could cut to the heart of the matter with a few words, as he did that night, but what he said also cut straight to my own heart.

We went through another night of torment, just as we had done when Marie died. There was no rest, no sleep, nowhere to escape. There was nothing but disbelief, and dread. I pleaded with God – why Peter, why us, what had we done to deserve this? I did not even have enough energy or composure to utter a silent prayer.

Perhaps you too have been thrust down deep into this valley of death, perhaps you, too, have been pleading with God. At such a time when you cannot find your own words, or any words, of comfort, you may find an echo of your unspoken thoughts in the words of the Psalms. They are full of raw, honest emotion, and this may bring you help. These are the words that came to me in the middle of one of my darkest of dark nights, only hours after Peter died:

> Out of the depths have I cried unto thee, O Lord.
>> Lord, hear my voice: let thine ears be attentive to the voice of my supplications . . . I wait for the Lord, my soul doth wait, and in his word do I hope.
>> My soul waiteth for the Lord more than they that watch for the morning: I say, more than they that watch for the morning.

Psalm 130

I also thought of the words of David, lamenting in deep torment, like us: 'O my son Absalom, my son, my son Absalom! would God I had died for thee, O Absalom, my son, my son!' We had lost our only son. My concern, too, was for Ingrid, and for Eloise, then eleven, and Judith, only two years younger. In the midst of all my heartbreak and despair, one thought alone kept me going – I knew that God had helped me through Marie's death, and that the same God would carry me through this time.

Peter's Funeral

Peter's funeral was no easier than Marie's. Logically you would think that having gone through one awful experience, we would have learned something, even if only the basic instinct of self-protection from pain. But it's not like that. The agony of the loss of a second child is just as excruciating as the first, or any other.

There was the same sense of shock and loss, though the circumstances were different. When Marie died, I was with her. Peter died almost alone, without any members of his family present, lying by the roadside in the darkness of a winter's night. I could not bring my mind even to think of that.

Marie's funeral was held in the full glare of publicity, amid the communal shock following the Enniskillen bomb. Peter's death was more private. It was the result of just another road accident, though the victim happened to be our only son. But because Gordon was so well known, allied to the circumstances of Peter's death, there was widespread media interest.

This time it was also different in that we issued a brief family statement to the media and then retreated into our own privacy. The media, to be fair, respected this and they left us to grieve in private, though understandably there was a large media presence outside the church. I sympathize very much with people who, because of their position, have to grieve not only privately, but also in the public gaze. We were given great support from the public, but it is hard enough to get through the dreadful day of the funeral without also having to try to put on a good face for the outside world.

On the day of Peter's funeral, I was worried about Gordon. He looked well, and spoke graciously to the many people who offered condolences in our home, or in the church and at the graveside. But I knew that he was churning inside, and he was very agitated. Just before the funeral he asked a good friend of ours if the family should go to the Caribbean for Christmas. He said that 'the girls' would need such a break, but we all knew that he was the one who really needed to get away.

The church was full of public dignitaries from Northern Ireland and the Irish Republic. Before the service we were introduced privately to President Mary Robinson, who was as fond of Gordon as he was of her. Her genuine sympathy and her quiet calmness were a source of strength to all of us. I admired her so much as a woman and as a President.

The funeral service was not easy for us, but it gave me comfort and hope. We all knew how we would have to face the lonely days and nights ahead simply trusting in Jesus, our help and guide. One of the hymns, which was chosen by Ingrid, brought that home to me:

> Simply trusting every day
> Trusting through a stormy way
> Even when my faith is small
> Trusting Jesus, that is all.
>
> Trusting as the moments fly
> Trusting as the days go by
> Trusting Him whate'er befall
> Trusting Jesus, *that is all*.

Page Stites

I also found comfort in the wonderful Resurrection hymn 'Thine be the Glory' originally written in French by Edmond Louis Budry and translated by Richard Hoyle,

No more we doubt thee, glorious Prince of Life;
Life is naught without thee: aid us in our strife;
Make us more than conquerors, through thy deathless
    love;
Bring us safe through Jordan to thy home above:
Thine be the Glory, risen conquering Son,
Endless is the victory thou o'er death hast won.

I have sung that hymn at many funerals, and it always brings me a surge of hope and reassurance about the life everlasting, but never more so than on that day when we said farewell to Peter.

My Son, My Son

When a child dies, it is an immense family tragedy. The suffering is deep and wide, and unfathomable in its intensity. There is no question of grieving more or less for a favoured child. The pain hits you like a hammer blow, and the dull ache of the pain goes on and on. I don't believe that any child is special to the exclusion of others. You love them all individually. But in all honesty, Peter had a special place in my heart. It's something I have never tried to rationalize or explain. When I think about it, he was maybe special because he was my only son. That link was intensified because I had lost our first son Richard shortly after his birth, but even though that was many years ago, I never ever forgot him. I know the pain of all parents who lose a baby in childbirth. Some people cannot even talk about it, long, long afterwards. You never get over it.

Peter and I got on well together. I brought out his soft side, perhaps more than Gordon, but strangely I was stricter with him than his father. Gordon indulged Peter, and I know that he would have given him his last penny. Though Peter and I were close, we had many a head-to-head encounter. He was charming and thoughtful, but he could also be stubborn. I did not give in to him as easily as Gordon!

Peter was also attentive. I loved the way he used to visit me every day when Gordon was away, just to check that I was all right. I also treasured the fact that he would confide in me about his business, and ask my advice about design and colour combinations. At the back of my mind I always thought that he would be there, with his strength and thoughtfulness. I even breathed a sigh of relief that I would be able to turn more and more to Peter in my old age.

Suddenly that was all gone. The ground had collapsed beneath my feet. Where once I had seen a rock, now there was only a gaping hole, an abyss. I just could not face life without the prospect of seeing him again. One part of my mind knew that he was gone, never to return to me in the old, familiar way. Yet another part of me refused to give him up. I suppose I was in a kind of denial, but I found comfort in words and messages which suggested that he had not really gone.

I understand if you feel that way too. It's a very human emotion, trying to cling on to someone we have loved so deeply that he or she is a part of our own life, our own body. I wrote the following words in my notebook about Peter. I do not know from where I have taken them, but they helped me greatly when I wanted to cling on to him, and to avoid the stark reality which I knew, in the depths of my being, was the cold truth.

> I cannot say and will not say
> That he is dead – he is just away
> With a cheery smile and a wave of the hand
> He has wandered into an unknown land
> And left us dreaming, how very fair
> It needs must be
> Since he lingers there
> In the love of here
> Think of him still
> As the same I say
> He is not dead
> He is just away.

On Loan

Peter was special to us and we thank God for him, for all the love and happiness he brought to our lives. He enriched us in so many ways and our memories of him are precious and personal.

At the same time, I am deeply conscious of all the other parents who have lost children, not only in the Northern Ireland Troubles, but also as a result of illness or road accidents. Their loss is also heart-breaking.

Sometimes in our search for consolation, it is helpful to realize that our child did not *belong* to us, in the sense that we owned this fresh, unique human being who had his or her own way to make in the world. In fact, our child was *on loan* to us for a short period, during which time we had a priceless opportunity to help mould this little life for good and to set the footsteps on the right path for the journey of life.

The hardest part, however, was having to realize that it was only a temporary loan, and not permanent, and it was beyond human endurance to be asked to give it up. This point was brought home to me by a poem which was sent by the mother of one of Peter's friends who had died just a few weeks before him. I hope that you will find the words helpful.

Prayer for Consolation

'I'll lend you for a little while,
A child of mine,' God said,

'For you to love the while he lives
And mourn for when he's dead.
It may be six or seven years
Or forty-two or three;
But will you, till I call him back,
Take care of him for me?
He'll bring his charms to gladden you, and should his stay be brief
You'll have his lovely memories as a solace for your grief.
I cannot promise he will stay since all from earth return;
But there are lessons taught below I want this child to learn.
I've looked the whole world over in my search for teachers true,
And from the things that crowd life's land, I have chosen you,
Now will you give him all your love, nor think the labour vain?
Nor hate me when I come to take this lent child back again?'
I fancied that I heard them say: 'Dear Lord, Thy will be done;
For all the joys thy child will bring the risk of grief we'll run.
We'll shelter him with tenderness. We'll love him while we may
And for the happiness we've known forever grateful stay.
But should thy angels call for him much sooner than we planned
We'll brave the bitter grief that comes
And try to understand.'

Talk About It

If you are bereaved, talk about it, and encourage others to do the same. Some people cannot handle that, but usually I find it's the person who has not been bereaved who is unable to talk about death. Sometimes this is the result of a well-meaning but misplaced kindness. The visitor or well-wisher believes that those who have been bereaved cannot bear to talk about the loved one who has gone. It's almost as if they never existed.

This is not helpful. On the contrary, it can cause the bereaved person even more distress. The fact is that they do want to talk about their loved one, about his or her kindness or foibles, eccentricities or sense of humour, and sometimes about all these aspects, and more. It is a way of keeping the memory of the loved one alive. A willingness to speak about the unspeakable, literally death, helps to rob it of its sting, and in conversation the departed person is remembered with affection and with respect for his or her humanity.

Sometimes the bereaved person has to take the lead and to encourage others to talk. In our family we never found any difficulty talking about Marie. I tell my grandchildren lots of stories about her. Equally now about Gordon and Peter. They are thought of daily, and spoken of frequently, at our family gatherings.

This sense of the familiarity of a loved one beyond the valley of death is well captured in this writing entitled 'Togetherness'. Copies were sent to me by many people, although it was months before I could concentrate or appreciate the contents. I would like to share it with you now, if you are able and ready to do so. If not, return to it later when you have more strength and time to appreciate its layered depths.

Death is nothing at all – I have only slipped away into the next room. Whatever we were to each other, that we are still. Call me by my old familiar name, speak to me in the easy way which you always used. Laugh, as we always laughed at the little jokes we enjoyed together. Play, smile, think of me, pray for me. Let my name be the household word that it always was. Let it be spoken without effort. Life means all that it ever meant. It is the same as it ever was; there is absolutely unbroken continuity. Why should I be out of your mind because I am out of your sight? I am but waiting for you, for an interval, somewhere very near just around the corner. All is well. Nothing is past; nothing is lost. One brief moment and all will be as it was before – only better, infinitely happier and for ever – we will all be one together with Christ.

Henry Scott Holland[1]

Different People – Different Pain

When death comes to a family, it is a mistake to believe that everyone grieves in the same way. That's what I found out about our family. We all felt the pain, but we were all different in our reactions to it.

It is a particular mistake to assume that your spouse or partner will feel exactly the way you do. If you are fortunate in having a good relationship, you will be able to share a great deal together. Sometimes if the relationship has become less than it might have been, the trauma of a child's death may help you find each other again. It is important to remember, however, that each person in a partnership and in a family needs his or her own space to come to terms with the death of the person they loved deeply.

Gordon and I talked endlessly about the deaths of Marie and of Peter. On long car journeys we would go over it, ask why it happened, think about how it had changed our lives. Sometimes such talk did not seem to do any good, but at least we cleared the air, we shared our grief, and it was a kind of therapy.

However, we needed our own space. I coped in my own way as best I could. So did Gordon. He used to go off on his own to the cemetery to look at the graves, and he would come back and say to me, 'Joan, that place is a terrible, sad sight.' There was very little I could add to that, but I knew that it was his way of coping.

I knew also that Ingrid was doing her best, and the little girls.

Gordon used to visit them and he would say, 'Whatever is going to become of these women down there?' He always referred to them all as 'these women'.

I was also aware that Julie-Anne was grieving deeply. She had her own husband, John, and family, but she missed her sister and brother, and she had to struggle to come to terms with their loss. There was no easy way for any of us.

It is also important to realize that all your family members will grieve at their own pace. The best you can do is to be aware of this, to allow each member his or her own space, and to give comfort when it is needed, just as the others will give the same comfort to you in your need.

I often read with benefit the following prayer for the members of our family, each of whom was touched and affected individually by Peter's passing.

Teach us, O Father, to trust Thee with life and with death
And (though this is harder by far)
With the life and death of those that
are dearer to us than our life

Teach us stillness and perfect peace
In thy perfect will
Deep calm of soul, and content
In what Thou wilt do with these lives Thou hast given

Teach us to wait and be still
To rest in Thyself
To hush this clamorous anxiety,
To lay in Thine arms all this wealth Thou hast given

Thou lovest these souls that we love
With a love as far surpassing our own
As the glory of noon surpasses the gleam of a candle
Therefore will we be still
And trust in Thee

J. S. Hyland[8]

Lonely – but Not Alone

❧✿❧

Even with the benefit of friends and of words of comfort, written or spoken, grief makes you feel isolated. This feeling will come suddenly, sometimes after a sight or a sound or a piece of music which reminds you of your loved one. At other times you will feel lonely for no apparent reason. You may be in a crowd, you may be busy with some task, you may be walking along the road – and suddenly you feel utterly lonely, just as lonely as that first moment when you faced the numbing reality of the death of your loved one.

You might find this shocking, or worrying, but it is all part of the grieving and of the healing process. Sometimes you will feel so lonely that you feel you cannot go on. There is a difference, however, between feeling lonely and in being totally alone. This is brought out by the following words which are familiar to most of us. Many kind people sent me copies of this famous passage. I read it and re-read it during those times when I feel utterly deserted, and it helps to lift my spirits.

> One night a man had a dream. He dreamed he was walking along the beach with the LORD. Across the sky flashed scenes of his life. For each scene, he noticed two sets of *footprints in the sand*; one belonging to him, and the other to the LORD.
>
> When the last scene of his life flashed before him, he looked back at the footprints in the sand. He noticed many times along the path of his life there was only one

set of footprints. He also noticed that it happened at the very lowest and saddest times of his life.

This really bothered him and he questioned the LORD about it. 'LORD, you said that once I decided to follow you, you'd walk with me all the way. But I have noticed that during the most troublesome times in my life there is only one set of footprints. I don't understand why when I needed you the most you would leave me.'

The LORD replied, 'My precious, precious child, I love you and I would never leave you. During your times of trial and suffering, when you see only one set of footprints, it was then that I carried you.'

Diana – an English Rose

Shortly after the Enniskillen bomb, Prince Charles and Princess Diana visited the town to meet the families of those who had died, or had been injured. During the reception, I talked to Prince Charles. He was most gracious and totally sincere. I felt that he really cared. Gordon met Princess Diana, and he was very taken with her, not only because she was a beautiful young woman, but also because of her great empathy with the relatives.

Later on, we experienced the total caring of the Princess. When Peter died, Gordon received the following hand-written letter:

> News of the latest tragedy to befall your family will have filled millions of people with a depth of sympathy they feel unable to express. I am no better able to tell you of my feelings for you all, and so to write only in the hope that now – or in the future – this thought (and all those prayers) may be of some small comfort.
>
> With love from Diana.

Just six months later, after Gordon's death, I too received a personal letter from the Princess. She wrote:

> Like millions of others, I was deeply saddened to read of your husband's sudden and tragic death. No words of mine will make his loss any easier to bear, but I hope that at some brief moment in the future this inadequate

message of sympathy – and the many more which will be unspoken – may be of comfort.

I felt privileged to have met Gordon and very enriched even by such a brief acquaintance. His reward will surely be great.

With love from Diana

These letters show the depth of feeling from a beautiful woman who cared deeply about other people in need. I treasure her letters, and the quiet thoughtfulness of a young woman who herself experienced such sadness and whose life ended in tragedy. When I think of her, I am reminded of an extract from *Just Listen to This* by Elizabeth Urch:

A Sundial Motto

Time is
Too slow for those who Wait
Too swift for those who Fear
Too long for those who Grieve
Too short for those who Rejoice

But for those who Love
Time is not.[9]

The Land of Lost Content

There is great healing in Nature. Just as I remembered how the snowdrops played an important part in the beginning of my healing after Marie's death, I also realized how much Peter had loved scenery, mountains and lakes. Some lines by A. E. Housman evoke in me memories of the nature which Peter loved, and the days of innocence we can never recapture.

> Into my heart an air that kills
> From yon far country blows:
> What are those blue remembered hills,
> What spires, what farms are those?
>
> That is the land of lost content,
> I see it shining plain,
> The happy highways where I went
> And cannot come again.[10]

That last verse speaks to my heart with such a sense of regret, but we cannot look back with unhappiness all the time. There are happy memories too. Peter loved fishing, since he had been a wee boy going out with his grandfather, who was a champion and fished for Ireland in his day. Peter loved the scenery at lovely Glen-Car, which is mentioned by William Butler Yeats in his poem 'The Stolen Child'.

> Where the wandering water gushes
> From the hills above Glen-Car,

In pools among the rushes
That scarce could bathe a star,
We seek the slumbering trout
And, whispering in their ears,
Give them unquiet dreams:
Leaning softly out
From ferns that drop their tears
Over the young streams . . .[11]

Thinking of the sights and sounds that our loved ones especially enjoyed, visiting places that they cherish, can grow into beautiful memories.

Letters

One of the best ways to send, or receive, words of sympathy is in a letter. Some people hesitate to write because they do not know what to say or how to say it. So they keep putting it off until it is almost too late. A letter of sympathy after a bereavement should be written and sent soon after the person has died, unless there is a good reason for not doing so – for example, if you have been abroad for some time and have only recently heard the sad news. Generally, the longer you wait, the harder it is to write. Sooner or later you will meet the bereaved person, and if you have not written a letter you will end up by apologizing and saying something like, 'I meant to write to you but . . .'

As someone who has been bereaved not once but three times in a relatively short period, I did not look for letters of sympathy nor did I think anything less of those people who did not write. I know that sometimes we do not carry out our best intentions.

However, one thing I have learned about expressing sympathy is the importance of putting pen to paper. Your letter need not be long, nor elaborate, nor should you worry about coining fine phrases. The best letters are written from the heart, in everyday language, and with an inner sympathy which the person will understand. The following letter from friends of ours, the Reverend Ivan and Margaret Hull, is a good example. To me it is a little gem which I read on the many occasions when I felt down and was mourning Peter. It always lifted my spirits.

Dearest Gordon and Joan,

Margaret joins with me in saying how sorry we were to hear of the sudden and tragic death of Peter.

His death was something just 'out of the blue' as it was completely unforeseen and without warning. He was such a lovely young man who loved his family.

Peter's death has come as a severe blow to you both and after Marie, it only intensifies the pain you both have come through. We are only human and finite and it is natural for us to ask why? But there are mysteries in life for which there are no immediate answers. Often we must wait for that day when mysteries are resolved and questions answered, and then we will understand how some things fit into a greater plan. Till then we are called to persevere in childlike trust in our heavenly Father. One thing you have already proved is that God gives grace to his children to help them cope. He will not fail you.

It is a source of comfort to know that when we die, however we die, believing in Jesus, then we are safe in the hands of Jesus. Peter and Marie are together with the Lord and one day you will be reunited with them. God's comfort reaches you also through the prayers of many friends, many known to you and many unknown. So may the Lord hold up your heads and keep you going, knowing that he walks with you.

Our prayers reach out to Ingrid and the children Eloise and Judith, and to Peter's sister Julie-Ann.

May the Lord embrace you all in his arms of love and give you His peace.

Maybe you, too, have received a letter like this, and if so, you are blessed. Or perhaps, it may be your turn to write to someone who is bereaved and in need of words of comfort. Just sit down and write words from your heart.

Remembering

One of the most important aspects of bereavement is that we keep remembering the loved one we have lost and that they are talked about, included in conversations, kept alive by memory and by affection and respect. In that sense they will never really die to us.

Inevitably these will be sad thoughts and conversations, particularly at the beginning. Yet, almost by a miracle, as time goes on you will also remember some of the happy moments, the good times spent together, the stories you shared, that special meeting-place which meant so much to you both, that ridiculous hat which he or she wore, their favourite food, that corny joke which you both laughed at despite yourselves, that dog-eared old book which you both treasured – the thousand and one things that bound your lives together. These are the golden memories, and once they begin to come, you might even be able to smile again, not just with your lips and eyes, but also deep in your heart.

This poem by Christina Rossetti, who also captured the darkness of the sleeping earth in her hymn 'In the Bleak Midwinter', underlines here the importance of remembering without sadness.

> Remember me when I am gone away,
> Gone far away into the silent land;
> When you can no more hold me by the hand,
> Nor I half turn to go, yet turning stay.

Remember me when no more day by day
You tell me of our future that you plann'd:
Only remember me; you understand
It will be late to counsel then or pray.

Yet if you should forget me for a while
And afterwards remember, do not grieve:
For if the darkness and corruption leave
A vestige of the thoughts that once I had,
Better by far you should forget and smile
Than that you should remember and be sad.

Christina Rossetti (1830–94)

Farewell

Bereavement has been described as untying thousands of little knots, cutting loose from the innumerable ways in which our lives are bound up together, but you never say farewell to your loved one, in an absolute sense. As long as you live you will never forget them. You will always remember their voice, their smile, their laughter, their sayings, their silences, their love.

There are times also when memories are not enough, when the separation seems too great, and you are too weak and too frightened even to pray.

At such a time it is important to hold on to the comforting words of St Paul in his Epistle to the Romans, chapter 8, verses 26 and 27:

> In the same way, the Spirit helps us in our weakness. We do not know what we ought to pray for, but the Spirit himself intercedes for us with groans that words cannot express. And he who searches our hearts knows the mind of the Spirit, because the Spirit intercedes for the Saints in accordance with God's will.

We are never alone when we grieve, and when we feel that God is furthest away, it is at that very time that he is closest. When we cannot find words to pray, the Holy Spirit prays for us.

As time passes, you will receive not only spiritual help but also the strength to hand over your loved one on their spiritual journey to God, the centre and power of all life. The following is a prayer of comfort I use when a deep longing for Peter, and for Marie and Gordon, sweeps over me.

We give them back to Thee dear Lord, who gavest them to us. Yet as Thou didst not lose them in giving, so we have not lost them by their return.

Not as the world givest, givest Thou, O Lover of Souls. What Thou givest Thou takest not away, for what is Thine is also ours if we are Thine. And life is eternal and love is immortal and death is only an horizon and an horizon is nothing save the limit of our sight.

Lift us strong Son of God, that we may see further; cleanse our eyes that we may see more clearly: draw us closer to Thyself that we may know ourselves to be nearer to our loved ones who are with Thee. And while Thou dost prepare a place for us, prepare us also for that happy place, that where they are and Thou art, we too may be for evermore.

Bishop Brent (1862–1929)

GORDON

An Ordinary Hero

Following Peter's funeral, Gordon threw himself into a frenetic round of engagements as if he was trying to blot out through his activities the awful reality of his son's tragic death. He travelled all over Ireland to fulfil a long series of speaking commitments to groups of people involved in reconciliation work; he spoke regularly and powerfully in the Irish Senate in Dublin; he allowed himself to be interviewed by journalists from all over the world; and he took every opportunity possible to speak out against violence and to urge the Irish people – and particularly the politicians and the paramilitaries – to work for peace.

His family and friends knew only too well that he was in danger of burning himself out. His daughter Julie-Anne tried in vain to persuade him to take life easier. So, too, did the then Irish Prime Minister Albert Reynolds, who earlier had offered him a seat in the Senate as an independent member. He said to Gordon, 'You are doing a fine job, but slow down a bit!' Gordon listened politely, but carried on as before.

Despite the pressures, Joan felt that – paradoxically – he was in better shape physically than he had been, at least up until Peter died. 'He had been devastated by Marie's death, but after a period of ill-health he had begun to put on weight, and he was learning very gradually to cope with the pain of bereavement. But the death of Peter shattered him. On the surface he appeared in control, though at times over-exerted, but perhaps deep down he had lost the will to keep going on, even the will to live. He had been through so much.'

Gordon died peacefully on a beautiful summer morning in June 1995. He was sixty-seven. Joan was away in Galway, on a visit with a party of Enniskillen musicians and school-children. He had been waiting at his home for Julie-Anne to pick him up and take him to her house in Moira, prior to an evening engagement in Belfast. When she arrived at her parents' house, she found that the doors and windows were lying open, and that he was not answering her call.

Fearing the worst, she went upstairs. She found him lying on his bed, as if he had simply fallen asleep. He had placed his glasses on the bedside table. Perhaps he had felt tired or a little unwell, and had gone upstairs to lie down, which he had sometimes done in the past. Only a few years earlier he had survived the horrendous Remembrance Day explosion at the Cenotaph in Enniskillen. It was ironic that on a lovely summer morning he passed away peacefully in the serenity of his own home. The last years of his life had been filled with so much stress and activity, and with a deep inner pain. But when the end came, it was gentle and peaceful. He had given his all.

His sudden death, from a stroke, was the final chapter in a remarkable story of an ordinary man whose extraordinary personal and Christian response to a trauma, which had torn apart his family and deeply shocked the whole community, had impressed people all over the world. But it was also the beginning of yet another nightmare for Joan, who was still struggling to cope with the deaths of Marie and Peter. It was almost too much for any human being to be asked to bear.

Darkness – Again

On the morning Gordon died, I heard the news very soon afterwards from a colleague in Galway, where I was playing the piano with a group of musicians and Enniskillen school-children. We were giving a concert in a supermarket, of all places, and I had just finished a trio of items with the Collegiate School Choir. At the end the conductor, Bob Quick, came to me, held my hands and told me directly, 'I'm sorry to give you terrible news. Gordon had a heart attack and has died at home.' It must have been awful for Bob to have had to pass on such a message. Sometimes the best way is to be direct, because the dreaded truth has to sink in sooner or later. My mind was in a whirl. I suppose I was doing the right things, and not panicking in public, but when someone offered me tea I noticed that my hands were shaking. I could hardly hold the cup.

What I remember most clearly, apart from the feeling of shock and dread, was the kindness of people. The Galway police were gentle and understanding, as they drove me towards Claremorris where I had arranged to meet Julie-Anne. We were given a lift home by Peter Little, whose father had driven Gordon home part of the way on the night Peter died.

I could not help saying to myself, 'Here we are on a beautiful summer's day, but this awful darkness has descended again.' In the midst of the tension and grief, the practicalities of the situation crossed my mind. 'There's another funeral to plan,' I said to myself, but then felt a surge of relief – 'Peter will be a great help.' To my horror I remembered that Peter was dead too.

It's odd how your mind plays tricks with you at such moments.

I remember returning to the house and being greeted by a blur of people. It was good to feel their warmth and support. But the most important person of all was missing. There was no cheery greeting from Gordon – 'Well, how did it go in Galway?' There was no big smile for me in the hallway. I felt bereft and broken. It was one of the loneliest moments of my life.

The one thing I dreaded was going up to see Gordon, lying dead on our bed. Yet I couldn't bear not seeing him. Julie-Anne, who herself had suffered so much, tried to protect me and told me not to go in. But I had to see him. Once I was inside the room, the feeling of dread lifted from me. Gordon looked so peaceful. He had done so much for peace and reconciliation, he had suffered so much, and he had achieved so much. As I looked at his face, and his silent, almost sleeping, figure, the words came to me, 'Mission accomplished.'

I left the room, and then I went back in again, alone. I thought of all we had been through, of our thirty-nine years together, of the happy times and the tragedies of Marie and Peter. In the midst of all these turbulent emotions I thanked God for all He had given us together, for His strength and inspiration in the good times and the bad.

I knew that the days ahead would be hard. There was so much to be done, to be gone through, to be endured, and I knew that I had very little strength left. In the midst of all my grief, weakness and despair, it was as if an emotional earthquake had shaken the foundations of my existence. I knew that my only strength came from God. I thought of those powerful words from Psalm 46, and they gave me comfort, and the courage to go on.

> God is our refuge and strength, a very present help in trouble.
> Therefore will not we fear, though the earth be

removed, and though the mountains be carried into the midst of the sea . . .

Be still, and know that I am God . . .

The Lord of hosts is with us; the God of Jacob is our refuge.

Mission Accomplished

Gordon's funeral was different from those of Marie and Peter. Theirs had been a long agony, saying 'Farewell' to young ones cut off in their prime. They had so much to give, and so much still to accomplish. And the sense of hurt, even of unfairness, was overwhelming.

Gordon's funeral was unbearable in its own way. This was the end of our long partnership, the physical confirmation that we would not meet again, on this side of the grave. Yet, there was also a feeling of gratitude, almost a sense of thankfulness for what Gordon had achieved, for a good life, well lived.

The range of people in the large congregation bore testimony to that fact. There were Roman Catholics sitting side by side with Protestants, which would not have surprised Gordon, but which would have warmed his heart. His life had been devoted to better understanding between the two main communities.

At the funeral there were also leading public representatives from North and South. They included President Mary Robinson, whose inner strength and sympathy touched me greatly as she had done at Peter's funeral; Lady Mayhew, the wife of the Northern Ireland Secretary of State, and leading political figures including the Irish Premier John Burton and the former Premier Albert Reynolds, who had given Gordon the opportunity to take part in public life. He said to me, 'I am so sorry for your loss, but I believe that Gordon killed himself by doing so much. I advised him to ease off, but he would not listen to me.'

Representatives from most of the main political parties in

Northern Ireland were present, including Mitchell McLaughlin, representing Sinn Fein, the political wing of the Republican movement whose armed representatives had killed Marie and all the others as a result of the Enniskillen bomb. It cannot have been easy for him to attend, but I know that he was made welcome, and I was pleased. Gordon would not have had it any other way. There were many representatives of the Unionist community who attended in a personal capacity. What mattered to me most was that Gordon's true friends were at the funeral.

Once again I felt comforted by the words and the music of the service. I was conscious, too, of the burden on Julie-Anne and the other members of the family. It was also a very strange experience. Unusually for Ireland it was an intensely hot day, and all the men in the packed church had taken off their jackets, and were in their shirt-sleeves. It was almost surreal. Outside the sun was shining, the world was going about its business, and here we were paying our last respects to Gordon in our family church.

It was all so sudden, so final, and so unfair, though in a different way to the deaths of Marie and Peter. Why wasn't Gordon allowed to slip into retirement, and to spend his last years with his beloved grandchildren? All kinds of thoughts were running through my head, but what I remembered most of all, and which gave me strength, were the words of a Charles Wesley hymn, which was one of Gordon's favourites:

> Jesu, Lover of my soul,
> Let me to Thy bosom fly,
> While the nearer waters roll,
> While the tempest still is high;
> Hide me, O my Saviour, hide,
> Till the storm of life is past;
> Safe into the haven guide,
> O receive my soul at last!

Other refuge have I none;
Hangs my helpless soul on Thee;
Leave, O! leave me not alone,
Still support and comfort me.
All my trust on Thee is stayed,
All my help from Thee I bring;
Cover my defenceless head
With the shadow of Thy wing.

During the service I knew in my heart that the words of that hymn were true – the storms of life were past for Gordon, his soul had been brought safely into God's haven, and the shadow of God's wing would cover all our heads which were so totally defenceless.

Stepping Stones

Even though you have experienced bereavement, and perhaps more than once (as I have done in tragic circumstances), it is never the same the next time. You think that you know what to do, but in the event you are overwhelmed once again by a feeling of deep pain, and of lasting loss. It's as if yet another part of you has been brutally torn away.

Maybe you feel the same in your bereavement, and you just don't know how to face the future. My advice is to try to take one day at a time. Don't worry about the long-term future, which will burden you down. Try not to dwell on the past, which has its own hurts and disappointments, and concentrate on the tasks at hand. If you do so, you will be given strength to cope, literally one day at a time.

It is also important to set yourself targets, but try to aim for little victories which you know you can achieve. After Gordon's death I found it hard to go out in public, even into a shop. But one day I plucked up courage, and did my shopping. It all went without a hitch. I remember thinking 'Gordon would be proud of me!' That might sound daft, to other people, but if you are going through a bereavement for the first time, or for more than the first time, I think you will understand.

I call these little targets and victories 'stepping stones', which help you to make your path from the desert of bereavement to the more familiar highways of normal life. But remember, it takes time.

After Gordon's death, I received many letters and messages

which helped me greatly. I particularly liked a poem by Michael Massey, a teacher from Kilkenny. It was passed on to me by Alan Dukes, a senior Member of the Irish Parliament, and a former colleague of Gordon's, who had received it from Mr Joe Cody, also of Kilkenny. Alan Dukes wrote, 'I find that the poem expresses very well the great respect and affection that so many people felt for Gordon.' I agree, and I also think that this lovely poem underlines the importance of taking first steps, big or small.

Stepping Stones
in memory of Gordon Wilson

News of your death slaps
cold as a wave into June;
shocks us as sudden death does
for we had come to know you
through your public pain,
had even felt a measure of guilt.

Down below the Dysart Bridge
I seek the gift of running water,
find it, too, where the Dinin
swirls and sparkles
among sun-washed stones.

But I remember the wettest winter
when muddy flood water exploded
over the rocky river bed
in an almighty rush to complete
the cycle: and I'm thinking now
of Marie's life cycle

and how it was cut short,
how you were heart-blasted,
how some felt cheated when you
did not seek an eye for a bloody eye,
but rose above the cold current:

a stepping stone, careworn smooth,
inviting tentative feet
to take the first step;
and there is need,
there is always need
of first steps and stepping stones.

Michael Massey

The Balm of Music

❧❧

All my life I have loved music, as a student and teacher, or just playing the piano for my own comfort and enjoyment. I have a baby grand in our living-room, and I often sit there and play to my heart's content, literally 'to content my heart'. There is a great power in music, and especially in what we call classical music.

In the early days after Gordon's death, I was not able to play, but I listened to classical music regularly. At the start I could only turn to Bach, Mozart and Beethoven. Someone reminded me recently of the old saying, 'When the angels talk to each other, they speak Beethoven and Bach. When they talk to God, they speak Mozart.'

I continued my role as choir-mistress in the local Methodist Church from 1977 until the year 2000. To my delight, the position was taken over by Ingrid. My work as choir-mistress helped to provide a purpose and a focus, and the choir will never know how important each member has been to me. Even today I continue to receive great comfort from music. I believe that it is the balm of the soul.

If you are not 'into' classical music, don't worry. Try to listen to whatever music brings you a sense of relaxation and peace. Sometimes you will find that what you think is 'popular' music has its roots in the classics. The important point is to listen, to relax and to enjoy. Music allows and helps us to live through the pain.

There let the pealing organ blow
To the full voiced choir below
In service high and anthems clear
As may with sweetness, through my ear
Dissolve me into ecstasies
And bring all Heaven before my eyes ...

John Milton

I think there must be a place in the soul all made of tunes of long ago.

Charles Ives

Make a large place in your life for music and it will bring you a priceless reward. All the desires of your heart will come closer as you become attuned to the rhythm and harmonies of life. In the hour of rest, music will uplift your spirit and give refreshment to every faculty of your being. In the hour of work you will rejoice in the strength and energy which music will bring you. In the hour of prayer, music will quicken the aspiration of your soul. In the hour of fellowship music will blend your spirit with others in unity and understanding.

From the organ loft of Whitfield's tabernacle

I also like the poem 'Music' by Walter de la Mare:

When music sounds, gone is the earth I know
And all her lovely things even lovelier grow
Her flowers in vision flame, her forest trees
Like burdened branches, stilled with ecstasies.

When music sounds out of the water rise
Nature whose beauty dims my leaking eyes.
Rapt in strange dream burns each enchanted face,
With solemn echoing stirs their dwelling-place.

When music sounds all that I was I am
Ere to this haunt of brooding dust I came
While from Time's woods break into distant song
The swift winged hours, as I hasten long.

Turmoil – and Peace

There are times during bereavement when you are at the mercy of your emotions. As the dull ache begins to wear away, you feel that you might be glimpsing a light at the end of the tunnel. Then something happens, and you crumple back into tears again. It might be the words of a hymn, or a line of poetry, or an anniversary, or just sheer loneliness at a time when everyone else seems to have someone to talk to.

Don't be afraid of those moments. They are natural steps in the healing process. Sometimes I was in utter despair, like the Psalmist, and at other times, in the quiet of a summer's evening, I felt a gentle peace stirring in my heart. It is important to remember, however, that one can follow the other with almost shocking intensity. So be prepared for swings in mood, but also for moments of peace, and of hope, despite the tears.

These two readings symbolize both the darkness of despair and the peace that will also come to you. They are both part of the varied tapestry of bereavement and of learning to trust life, and God.

The words of Psalm 6 are among the bleakest in the Bible, but they ring true to those of us who have been thrust deep into the pit of despair:

> O Lord, do not rebuke me in your anger
>   or discipline me in your wrath.
> Be merciful to me, Lord, for I am faint;
>   O Lord, heal me, for my bones are in agony.

My soul is in anguish.
  How long, O Lord, how long?

Turn, O Lord, and deliver me;
  save me because of your unfailing love.
No-one remembers you when he is dead.
  Who praises you from his grave?

I am worn out from groaning;
  all night long I flood my bed with weeping
  and drench my couch with tears.
My eyes grow weak with sorrow;
  they fail because of all my foes.

Away from me, all you who do evil,
  for the Lord has heard my weeping.
The Lord has heard my cry for mercy;
  the Lord accepts my prayer.
All my enemies will be ashamed and dismayed;
  They will turn back in sudden disgrace.

Just as dawn follows the darkest hour, peace and assurance
will arise from despair. This summer poem by Matthew Arnold
has given me great comfort:

The evening comes, the fields are still.
The tinkle of the thirsty rill,
Unheard all day, ascends again;
Deserted is the half-mown plain,
Silent the swaths! the ringing wain,
The mower's cry, the dog's alarms,
All housed within the sleeping farms!
The business of the day is done,
The last-left haymaker is gone.
And from the thyme upon the height,
And from the elder-blossom white

And pale dog-roses in the hedge,
And from the mint-plant in the sedge,
In puffs of balm the night-air blows
The perfume which the day foregoes.
And on the pure horizon far,
See, pulsing with the first-born star,
The liquid sky above the hill!
The evening comes, the fields are still.

The Spirit of Enniskillen

❧❦❧

Some good can come out of the darkest despair, and Gordon and I were so encouraged by the development of a number of positive initiatives, following the Enniskillen bomb. One of these was the establishment of the 'Spirit of Enniskillen' Bursaries which provided the means for selected young people to travel to areas of the world where others have been, and are, coping with community problems. The hope is that our young people will be able to relate to the community problems back home, and to learn from the experience.

The British Government provided £150,000 to start the scheme, and the investment was later increased to £180,000. The American Ireland Fund also helped by underwriting extra Bursaries each year. This work is very worthwhile, and I am so pleased that I am invited to the launch of the annual Bursaries. It is most encouraging to meet and to listen to the young people speaking about their experiences in the different countries they have visited. I was particularly delighted when my grand-daughter Eloise had the opportunity of going to Cyprus, by means of one of the Bursaries, and she was chosen on her own merit!

Another imaginative scheme is the Marie Wilson Voyage of Hope, whereby young Protestants and Roman Catholics from Northern Ireland visit Canada each year. Again this is not a holiday, but an opportunity for our young people to find out how people in another part of the world handle their community problems. In June each year I have the pleasure of meeting the young people who have gone on these visits, and I present each of them with a copy of the *Marie* book. I find that somewhat apprehensive young people who go to Canada come back assured, friendly, confident and at ease with one another. Significantly, they have a different attitude to the troubles here, and the whole experience broadens their outlook.

I know that the work of the 'Spirit of Enniskillen' Bursaries and of the Marie Wilson Voyage would gladden the heart of Gordon if he were alive to see it. This quote from one young person on a visit to Canada symbolizes the progress that is being made:

> When I was in Toronto someone asked me, 'With the peace process and the Good Friday Agreement do you not think that projects like this are no longer needed?' My answer is this: We have a chance to shape the future so that it will never be like what it was in the past, and it is through projects like this that we can come together and work together in the real world. On this trip we needed to rely on each other and I came to realize that as I sat with Joanne looking over the lake as the stars scattered the sky, it's a big world out there, and our friends are the only ones who will look out for us, and that no religious divide can defy friendship.

For the Good Times

People say that it is awful to lose a child, but the worst of all is to lose a partner. I can understand that. When your child dies, part of you also goes to the grave, but when you lose a husband, or a wife, you lose part of your own identity.

Gordon and I had been together for nearly forty years. We had a very happy marriage, but we had many a private set-to. Some people tell me that they have been married for forty years without a cross word, but I don't always believe them! Any relationship which grows and develops has its moments of testing. Gordon and I were both strong characters, and he did some things which drove me mad, as I am sure I did to him. But our 'ding-dongs' were always in private, and they never lasted. We had a rich and a close relationship, and I thank God for it.

After Gordon died I missed his companionship, his conversation and his sense of humour. When he went to the Irish Senate in Dublin he used to come back with great stories about the characters and the happenings there. Gordon was a great story-teller, and he made me roar with laughter. If you have been lucky in that way too, don't feel guilty about remembering the laughter and the fun. They are great healers. And don't forget to thank God for the good times.

Prayer for a Loved One Departed

You shared life with us
God give
Eternal life to you.

You gave your love to us
God give
His deep love to you.

You gave your time to us
God give
His eternity to you.

You gave your light to us
God give
Everlasting light to you.

Go upon your journey dear soul
to love,
Light, and life eternal.

Source unknown

Stand By Your Man

When someone close to you dies, you spend a long time thinking back on what made them the way they were. In the hurly-burly of daily life, you do not have the time to reflect enough on the deeper qualities of those to whom you were close. During bereavement there is an opportunity, indeed a compulsion, to reflect in this way. If you do this with a sense of gratitude for the best qualities in the loved one who has departed, this can be an important part of your healing process.

I remember Gordon as a big man, big in stature and big in heart. He lived reconciliation, not because it was the right thing to do, but because he believed totally that it was the only way to build bridges between individuals and communities. But most of all I remember his courage. It took great courage to move forward into the spotlight to answer questions from the media, who looked for a comment and sound-bite everywhere he went.

Gordon knew that this was resented by other people, including the relatives of some victims, and it grieved him. But he felt that he could not turn down any opportunity to speak out against violence.

It took enormous courage to confront the Provisional IRA and to meet them face to face. I was so frightened when he went to see them. I thought about all the horrible things that might happen – maybe he would end up lying dead in a ditch. I could not even think about doing what he did. But he had the courage to go into the lions' den, just like Daniel.

He showed courage, too, in taking a seat in the Irish Parliament. Many Northern Protestants resented this, including friends who thought he was letting the Unionist side down by doing so. We knew that people talked behind our backs, because in a small community that kind of comment always gets carried. It was hurtful, but we said nothing. The work Gordon was doing was too important to be sullied by personal animosities, and he was not a man to hold grudges.

Gordon personified courage of the highest order, and it was my privilege to back him up to the hilt, whenever and wherever I could. I knew more than anyone else the physical toll it was taking of him. He often said to me in private, 'Some people don't understand. I've been through *a bomb*.' But he never complained in public, he just did what he had to do. I have never known a more courageous or big-hearted man than my Gordon. I thank God for every memory of him. He is now at rest.

> The righteous perish,
>   and no-one ponders it in his heart;
> devout men are taken away,
>   and no-one understands
> that the righteous are taken away
>   to be spared from evil.
> Those who walk uprightly
>   enter into peace;
>   they find rest as they lie in death.
>
> Isaiah 57:1–2

Peace in Our Time

I remember Gordon's reaction when the first Provisional IRA cease-fire was announced. He was delighted that at last there was a possibility of permanent peace. The years since then have been difficult, and peace is not yet assured, but we seem to have made some progress. Like Gordon, I welcomed the 'cease-fire' for many reasons, not least because an end to violence would spare families the trauma which we and others had to experience.

Most people do not realize the depth of suffering which the victims and their families have gone through. In Northern Ireland many have become hardened to violence, after so long. But each shooting or maiming so deeply affects not only the victim, but his or her entire family, and circle of friends.

I just cannot understand the mentality of those who carry out the violence, or support it politically. What happens, unfortunately, is that those who bomb and shoot, or break people's bones with baseball bats and other bludgeons, go into a kind of self-denial where the victims are not 'real' people but representatives of the hated 'enemy', such as a policeman or soldier or a member of a paramilitary organization. And if the victim is a civilian, then the blame is laid on somebody else – the Government, or 'the other side', or past history.

All of this is so much hypocrisy. When a person is killed or maimed, it is human beings who are affected, fathers and mothers, sisters and brothers, sons and daughters – real flesh and blood. Marie was not just a statistic, nor were any of the other people killed or maimed. It was part of Gordon's mission in life, and also mine, to do everythng possible to bring an end to violence and misunderstanding.

This is also part of my continuing mission so that when peace finally comes it will make Marie's death seem less senseless, in the knowledge that she, and all the others, did not die in vain. One of Gordon's favourite hymns, by John Greenleaf Whittier, the New England poet and hymn-writer, describes eloquently and beautifully the vision of all those who work for peace in Northern Ireland. I hope that one day this vision will become a reality:

> Follow with reverent steps the great example
> Of Him whose holy work was doing good.
> So shall the wide earth seem our Father's temple,
> Each loving life a psalm of gratitude.
>
> Then shall all shackles fall: the stormy clangour
> Of wild war-music o'er the earth shall cease,
> Love shall tread out the baleful fire of anger
> And in its ashes plant the tree of peace.

> John Greenleaf Whittier (1807–92)

All Our Suffering Is One

In bereavement it is tempting to think that you are the only one who is suffering. The wounds are so deep and the distress so real that they could become all-enveloping. In such a condition it is hard to empathize with the sufferings of others, and harder still to reach out to them. The awareness of the pain of other people does not necessarily lessen your own, but it helps to put your grief in perspective when you are aware of the sea of suffering all around you, all over the world.

This was brought home to me on 10 October 1996, when I attended Westminster Abbey for a Service of Inauguration of the memorial stone to civilian victims of the twentieth century. I had been invited by the Dean of Westminster, the Very Reverend Michael Mayne, as a representative of the people of Northern Ireland, together with Mrs Maura Kiely from Belfast, whose son Gerard, a student, had been shot dead in the Troubles.

The stone, which stands outside the great West Door of the Abbey in full view of the public, was unveiled by Her Majesty the Queen, accompanied by the Duke of Edinburgh. It was a dry, autumn day with a cold wind, and the leaves swirling. Somehow, the atmosphere was symbolic of all the suffering which the service represented.

My daughter Julie-Anne accompanied me. The service was very beautiful, and the great organ reverberating round the Abbey stirred my soul. The singing of the choir was most uplifting.

During the service we processed to the great West Door and stood round the stone, which has the inscription 'Is it nothing to you, all you that pass by'. I stood beside Eldin Isovic, aged fourteen, who had lost both hands and the sight of both eyes during the Bosnian conflict. His father was with him, and I noticed that he cried quietly during the entire service. I felt my heart break for them both.

After the ceremony we had a buffet in the Jerusalem Chamber and all the visiting representatives and members of various humanitarian organizations were presented to the Queen and the Duke. It was a beautiful and memorable occasion. It was also sad, at various times during the service, yet I had a great sense of thankfulness for the Dean of Westminster's vision to have this historic stone placed in memory of victims of the twentieth century. It was a reminder to me, in my bereavement and perhaps also in yours, that all over the world, our suffering is one. If you happen to be in London, I recommend that you go to see it.

I shall never forget the singing of a hymn by Dietrich Bonhoeffer, and the sense of people drawing nearer to God in their distress. I was so moved that I asked the members of my church choir to sing it a month later, during the Remembrance Day service in Enniskillen:

> People draw near to God in their distress,
> pleading for help and begging peace and bread,
> rescue from guilt and sickness, nearly dead.
> Christian or not, all come in helplessness.

> People draw near to God in his distress:
> find him rejected, homeless, without bread,
> burdened with sin and weakness, nearly dead.
> Christians stand with God in his wretchedness.

> And God draws near to people in distress,
> feeding their souls and bodies with his bread;
> Christian or not, for both he's hanging dead,
> forgiving, from the cross, their wickedness.[12]

Good Out of Evil

When something terrible happens in your life, like the death of a loved one, it is hard to believe that any good can come from this personal tragedy. It is even harder to believe this if your child, and other human beings, died as a result of the work of men and women who planted and detonated a bomb. How *can* any good come from such evil?

For many years I looked with dread on the spot where the Enniskillen bomb had gone off. To me it repesented blood and tears, evil and suffering, maiming and death. With the passage of time, however, things change. Not so long ago, I attended a sod-cutting ceremony at the same site which will house a new £3 million Education and Arts Centre, in conjunction with the University of Ulster, the local council, the Arts Lottery Fund, and the European Community. Clergy from the local churches held a short prayer service, and there was a minute's silence in memory of those killed and injured in the Enniskillen explosion. Other relatives of the victims attended the ceremony. There was an atmosphere of sadness, but also of hope, and a recognition that good can indeed come out of evil.

At this stage of your bereavement, you might find this difficult to comprehend. But do not close your mind or heart to the possibility of what might blossom from unpromising circumstances. You will never forget the pain, but you might also be able to appreciate, one day, the beauty of the new growth which emerges from tragedy and despair. One day, reading my

Scripture Union daily Bible reading notes, I came across this challenging thought:

> When the time of testing comes and situations are against us, then comes the real opportunity for God to work in us those qualities of trust, patience and perseverance. When we acknowledge He is in control of every situation, then He can bring good out of evil and order out of political turmoil and social chaos.

Reaching Out

One of the most important things you can do in bereavement is to reach out to others. At the start this will be difficult, because you need to deal with your own grief. However, as time goes on you will notice others who have lost loved ones too.

You may hear about this from people in your immediate neighbourhood, or it may be news from an old school friend, or a newspaper report about a person or a family you had come to know. In such a situation you might consider writing a note of sympathy, or if you are well acquainted, you might make a phone call or a visit.

After Marie's death, Gordon and I were very aware of others who were going through a bereavement. When Peter died we were even more aware of this, partly as a result of the many people – including strangers – who took the trouble to write to us. Many of them had recently gone through a bereavement of their own.

After Gordon died, some people thought that I would have been keen to continue his mission in public. However, I prefer to work quietly in the background. I see my role as trying to help people in need, and at an appropriate time I contact those with whom I might be able to share my experiences of coping with bereavement.

I am particularly conscious of people in Northern Ireland who have lost a loved one through the Troubles, and I try to bring them comfort where possible. I normally write first, and if they express a wish to see me personally, I try to meet them.

Usually I bring with me a copy of the *Marie* book, which relates better than I can the ways in which our family tried to cope.

Sometimes there is little you can say, because the grief is so deep, but your physical presence, and the fact that you have also travelled through the valley of the shadow of death, seem to help. On such occasions, however, you must be sure that you have the strength to bring help to someone else. There is no point in breaking down in their presence, because of your own heartache, and adding to their burdens.

Thankfully I have always been given the strength when I need it, and I find that such visits in a strange way help me also. There is a truth in the old saying that a burden shared is easier to carry. But you must go in the right frame of mind, and before embarking on such a visit, I turn to the words of this lovely hymn by Kate Barclay Wilkinson (1859–1928), which helps me on my way.

> May the mind of Christ my Saviour
>   Live in me from day to day,
> By his love and power controlling
>   All I do or say.
>
> May the word of God dwell richly
>   In my heart from hour to hour,
> So that all may see I triumph
>   Only through his power.
>
> May the peace of God my Father
>   Rule my life in everything,
> That I may be calm to comfort
>   Sick and sorrowing.
>
> May the love of Jesus fill me,
>   As the waters fill the sea;

Him exalting, self-abasing,
    This is victory.

May I run the race before me,
Strong and brave to face the foe,
    Looking only unto Jesus,
        As I onward go.

Time Does Not Heal

People have often said to me that 'Time heals all.' I don't agree. It is fourteen years since Marie died, and the wound has not healed. It is the same for Peter and Gordon, and even for my tiny son Richard who died many years ago, shortly after he was born. No matter how much time passes, these wounds will never heal completely. Your life will not be the same as it was, and once you let this really sink in, it will be an important milestone in your healing process. This is something you cannot force, but it will come in time.

It is important to understand, however, that the passage of time does bring some benefits. The pain does ease a little, and some of the happy memories help you through the tearful days. Most important of all, however, is the fact that time teaches you how to cope, to face each day, to avoid some of the obvious reminders of what life used to be like, and feeling sorry for yourself.

I know that people mean it kindly when they say 'Time heals all.' From my experience, it doesn't, but it does teach you how to cope – provided you are willing to be taught and to move on. Part of the coping is to learn to appreciate even more the beauty of life all around, not only in nature, but also in poetry. There is a timeless beauty in these lines from 'Endymion', by John Keats, which has been a favourite since my schooldays, and which helps me to appreciate and to remember all the lovely things that have happened to me in my lifetime:

A thing of beauty is a joy for ever:
Its loveliness increases; it will never
Pass into nothingness, but still will keep
A bower quiet for us, and a sleep
Full of sweet dreams, and health, and quiet breathing.
Therefore, on every morrow, are we wreathing
A flowery band to bind us to the earth,
Spite of despondence, of the inhuman dearth
Of noble natures, of the gloomy days,
Of all the unhealthy and o'er-darkened ways
Made for our searching – yes, in spite of all,
Some shape of beauty moves away the pall
From our dark spirits. Such the sun, the moon,
Trees, old and young, sprouting a shady boon
For simple sheep; and such are daffodils
With the green world they live in; and clear rills
That for themselves a cooling covert make
'Gainst the hot season; the mid-forest brake,
Rich with a sprinkling of fair musk-rose blooms;
And such too is the grandeur of the dooms
We have imagined for the mighty dead,
All lovely tales that we have heard or read –
An endless fountain of immortal drink,
Pouring unto us from the heaven's brink.

All Shall Be Well

During bereavement it is essential to hang on to the vision of light at the end of the tunnel, no matter how hard this is. There are times when the darkness all but crowds out the light, when you do not want to hear advice from friends, when you want to stay in your own small corner, pull the covers over your head, and let the grief sweep over you.

At other times, you will need the company of friends, you will be able to hear words of wisdom not only with your ears but also with your heart, you will begin to notice small signs of hope, like a snowdrop, a child's smile, a beautiful sunset, or a task completed on your own. You will begin to notice small victories, not necessarily each day, but the gaps between such victories will grow less. And you will gradually move towards an inner reassurance that even though things will never be the same again, in the essentials of your remaining life, all will be well.

I know that people often wonder how I cope, after so much sorrow. I lean heavily on the spiritual strength from God, but I also get on with my daily life. I find great comfort in the activities and achievements of my family, and particularly my grandchildren.

I find fulfilment in my church life, and in the music of the choir at Enniskillen Methodist Church. I enjoy the company of my many friends who have stuck by me in my times of need, and of new friends who come into my life. I love long walks, despite my arthritis, and I continue to find great solace in the beauties of nature. I make myself busy in my home and garden. I also keep time for reflection, but thankfully I have far too much in my life to let me brood on the past.

Of course life will never be the same again, without Marie and Peter and Gordon. But I am learning to make the best of each day, and I am thankful that all is well, certainly as well as it can be. I know in a deep spiritual sense that despite what has happened, and the worst of what might happen, all shall be well in the wide embrace of God's care.

I regard it as a privilege that you have joined me in my journey through this little book, and if anything I have written has helped you, I will feel greatly rewarded. I will leave you with these wise and ancient words from Mother Julian of Norwich. They have been a lifeline to me in times of great need, and they have given me also a wonderful sense of hope and of calm.

Read these words over and over. Sink them deep into your subconscious mind, and write them on your hearts. God bless you!

> All shall be well
>   and all shall be well
> and all manner of thing
>   Shall be well.

Epilogue

After so many years, there are times – incredibly – when it all seems like a bad dream. I still can hardly believe that Marie, Peter and Gordon have gone. It's as if we had been walking along a road and gradually there are fewer of us, as each one disappears along the way. It is my great consolation, and the centre of my Christian faith, that I will see them again some day. As Gordon said after Marie's death, 'I don't have an answer, but there has to be a plan . . . It's part of a greater plan, and God is good. And we shall meet again.'

When I look back I also remember the positive things, not only about our family life, but also about the people who helped us through. I think of the security forces and the ambulance, medical and nursing staff who did so much for the injured and their families on the day of the Enniskillen bomb. Someone told me afterwards that it was an Army doctor who was in the ambulance carrying Marie to the hospital and he kept saying to the driver 'Faster, faster.' The driver replied, 'My foot is on the accelerator to the board. I can't go any faster.'

I will always be grateful to my friends and neighbours who rallied during our times of bereavement – those who made tea, who baked cakes and made sandwiches and, above all, who helped to bring comfort and strength. I also think about all the families of those who died or were injured. There has been so much suffering among all the communities in Northern Ireland, over so many years. So much bloodshed, so much pain and so much despair. At times I felt that my heart would break with it all.

Thank God, however, I have always been given strength when I needed it, and somehow I have got through, with the help also of family and friends. And now at the end of it all my mind turns to that lovely hymn by John Greenleaf Whittier (1807–92), which was one of Gordon's favourites.

These words underline the violence of 'our foolish ways', the need for the 'still dews of quietness' to end all our 'strivings, strain and stress', and the importance of heeding that 'still small voice of calm' which will help to guide us to the ways of permanent peace, not only in our land but also deep in our hearts. May God grant us his mercy and strengthen and pardon us all.

> Dear Lord and Father of mankind,
>   Forgive our foolish ways;
> Reclothe in us our rightful mind;
> In purer lives thy service find,
>   In deeper reverence, praise . . .
>
> Drop thy still dews of quietness,
>   Till all our strivings cease;
> Take from our souls the strain and stress,
>   And let our ordered lives confess
>   The beauty of thy peace.
>
> Breathe through the heats of our desire
>   Thy coolness and thy balm;
> Let sense be dumb, let flesh retire;
> Speak through the earthquake, wind and fire,
>   O still small voice of calm!

Acknowledgements

Every effort has been made to trace copyright ownership and the publisher would be grateful to be informed of any omissions.

1 Peter Scott, *Eye on the Wind*, (Hodder and Stoughton, 1977).
2 Elizabeth Urch, *Be Still My Soul*, (Lochalsh Publications, 1969).
3 'Zither Carol' by M. Sargent, from *Carol Praise*, ed. D. Peacock and M. Perry, (Marshall Pickering, 1992, permission sought).
4 From *Letters of Direction*, by Abbé de Tourville, (Dacre Press, 1939).
5 'Beauty' by John Masefield, from *A Pageant of English Verse*, (Longmans, 1949, permission sought).
6 From *The Woman Who Wrote Black Beauty: A Life of Anna Sewell*, by Susan Chitty, (Hodder and Stoughton, 1971, permission sought).
7 'Death is nothing at all', by Henry Scott Holland, original source unknown.
8 'Teach Us, O Father to trust Thee', by J. S. Hyland, in Leslie Weatherhead, *A Private House of Prayer*, (Arthur James, 1985).
9 From Elizabeth Urch, *Just Listen to This*, (Lochalsh Publications).
10 From A. E. Housman, *A Shropshire Lad*, (Penguin Classics, 1999, permission sought).

11 'The Stolen Child' by William Butler Yeats, from *A Pageant of English Verse*, (Longmans, 1949, permission sought).
12 'People draw near to God' by Dietrich Bonhoeffer, original source unknown.